# *fabulous* Fondues

*Appetizers, main courses & desserts*

## FRED KERNER

Sterling Publishing Co., Inc.
New York

Edited by Jeanette Green
Designed by Judy Morgan

**Library of Congress Cataloging-in-Publication Data**

Kerner, Fred, 1921–
    Fabulous fondues : appetizers, main courses & desserts / Fred Kerner.
      p. cm.
    Rev. ed. of: It's fun to fondue / by M. N. Thaler. © 1968.
    ISBN 0-8069-5489-2
    1. Fondue.  I. Kerner, Fred, 1921–  It's fun to fondue.  II. Title.
TX825.T47 2000
641.8'1—dc21                                  00–028508

10  9  8  7  6  5  4  3

Published by Sterling Publishing Company, Inc.
387 Park Avenue South, New York, N.Y. 10016
Revised and enlarged edition of *It's Fun to Fondue*
published by Centaur House © 1968 by M. N. Thaler;
enlarged as *Mad About Fondue* by Fred Kerner,
published by Irwin Publishing, Toronto, Canada © 1986 by Fred Kerner
© 2000 by Fred Kerner
Distributed in Canada by Sterling Publishing
℅ Canadian Manda Group, One Atlantic Avenue, Suite 105
Toronto, Ontario, Canada M6K 3E7
Distributed in Great Britain and Europe by Cassell PLC
Wellington House, 125 Strand, London WC2R 0BB, England
Distributed in Australia by Capricorn Link (Australia) Pty Ltd.
P.O. Box 6651, Baulkham Hills, Business Centre, NSW 2153, Australia
*Manufactured in the United States of America*
*All rights reserved*

Sterling  ISBN 0–8069–5489–2

*For Zachary, Stephen, and Robert*

# Contents

## THE BOOK THAT CREATED A FAD!

This book developed from a discussion with the late literary agent Anita Diamant some 35 years ago. Its initial publication reportedly was responsible for a North American "cooking fad" that has now returned for the third time since the mid-1960s.

A relative of Ms. Diamant's, an importer of kitchenwares, had acquired a large shipment of fondue pots but found that most buyers didn't know what they were! In our travels—she as literary agent and I as publishing executive—we had often enjoyed fondue meals (in Switzerland especially). She asked if I could devise a pamphlet to accompany the pots, telling how easy they were to use.

The original plan was for an eight-page pamphlet. But when I discovered the fascinating lore of fondue-making, as well as a trove of intriguing and tasty ways for preparing a fondue, it ended up with 48 pages—the booklet had grown to a book! Within a year, many thousands of fondue pots were sold—and the "pamphlet" sold more than 100,000 copies. The author was a certain M. N. Thaler, a pun on the word *Emmenthaler*—what Europeans call our more familiar "Swiss cheese." Of course, today more people are cheese sophisticates and readily recognize the Emmenthaler name as well as many other varieties of European cheese. Also, many urban and suburban food markets sell these imports.

Craig Claiborne, food writer for *The New York Times*, in an article in the newspaper's Sunday magazine entitled "Dish of Many Disguises," featured recipes from the book and proclaimed that "One of the food phenomena of the decade has been the zoom to popularity of fondue bourguignonne."

The popular cookbooks of the day did include a recipe for fondue. *Fannie Farmer* listed the traditional "Swiss Fondue" and three other "fondue" recipes: all baked-egg soufflé dishes. *The Good Housekeeping Cook Book* also carried the traditional recipe, plus a baked-egg dish. *The Joy of Cooking* carried only a definition of the baked-egg version.

Before the fondue fad of the late 1960s had run its course, the book had reached almost a million readers—and, surprisingly, more than 100,000 were sold in Switzerland!

A second round of fondue fascination hit North America in the 1980s—*The New York Times* again publicizing the phenomenon, this time in a travel-section article, "Fondue: A Swiss Classic." The book was enlarged to 96 pages, retitled *Mad About Fondue*, conforming to the publisher's "Mad About" series of cookbooks, and cumulative sales increased to more than 1,200,000 copies.

Now we are in the midst of the third wave of interest in fondue cooking. So here is *Fabulous Fondues*, enlarged anew with still more tasty, fun-to-make (and to eat) dishes.

Enjoy!

—*Fred Kerner*
*Toronto, June 2000*

# Introduction

## THE FONDUE IS A FUN-DO

The Swiss must have had us in mind when they invented fondue cooking. Nothing could be better tailored to our delight with informality than an eating occasion at which everyone is invited to "do it yourself."

Beside après-ski fires, at cocktail parties, and at dinner, guests gather—with fondue fork in hand—around a pot for what turns out to be an amusing party game and a delectable eating experience.

We've expanded on the Swiss invention. Instead of two traditional fondues—cheese and beef—we now use the fondue pot for everything from appetizers to extraordinary desserts.

While there is some dispute about the origin of the word *fondue*, there is none about the enjoyment fondue provides in both the fun and the flavor.

There is strong evidence that the word developed in the French-speaking part of Switzerland from the verb *fondre*, "to melt," and can be traced back as far as 1768. Some people in Switzerland, however, claim that the word means "to dip." Whether either is correct is immaterial. With the classic cheese fondue, you do both—you melt and you dip. Best of all, you partake of a meal that gives pleasure in every possible way.

Some people still tend to think of the fondue as haute cuisine. Actually it had humble beginnings. As have so many provincial dishes, it originated out of necessity and practicality. Since cheese has a tendency to become hard when stored for long periods, some practical, innovative—or even lucky—cook discovered that the hard cheese would melt and that dipping pieces of bread into it made a simple, delicious meal.

This type of fondue is not to be confused, of course, with the baked fondue made by soaking bread in a custard mixture of eggs and milk, adding cheese, and then baking until firm and golden. Nor has it anything to do with any of the vegetable side dishes—cooked to a pulp and sieved—that are also called fondues. The term *fondue* is also used for the dish of scrambled eggs, butter, and cheese—an appellation that *Larousse Gastronomique* once said was unjustifiable—the recipe for which is found in Brillat-Savarin's *Physiologie du goût*.

Some people have called the Fondue au Boeuf (page 62) a Fondue Bourguignonne, which is a misnomer in the strictest sense. First, nothing is melted; second, it is not a "bourguignonne" because the recipe does not use red wine, nor does it come from Burgundy.

Raclette, another version of fondue popular in Switzerland and France, uses small pans for melting cheese that is eaten with small boiled potatoes, pearl onions, and pickles. You can even buy raclette cheese for the purpose. In the Valais canton of Switzerland, another method involves simply holding a large chunk of cheese to the fire and scrapping off the softened parts as they melt.

Today, health-conscious chefs in restaurants across North America are creating fondue-style vegetable broths, dips, and sauces to be used with veggie dunkables.

Of course, there's more to a fondue than gustatory pleasure. Fondues are great icebreakers at parties, a parlor-game type of meal, and they're adaptable across the menu from hors d'oeuvre to dessert, from breakfast to dinner.

A fondue meal or party is appropriate almost any time, and as you become adept at the few simple rules of preparation and presentation, you will find new uses—and even variations—to delight your family and guests.

What are these simple rules? Let's list them quickly—running from cooking pointers and equipment to ingredients and etiquette.

## Integral Ingredients

**Cheese:** The cheese you use for a cheese fondue must be chosen with great care. For a basic fondue you need a well-matured Swiss cheese from Switzerland. Domestic Swiss, while tasty, is rarely mature enough to make a good fondue. We also suggest variations with stronger types of cheese in some recipes.

Cheese that is diced melts more smoothly and easily than cheese that is grated. Grated cheese tends to form lumps in the cooking process. If you are in a great hurry, shred the cheese.

**Wine:** While we suggest use of a number of wines in this book, basically you should use a light, sparkling, slightly acid wine. The Swiss insist that a Swiss wine is a must—something like a Neuchâtel, the acidity of which helps to liquefy the cheese and make it homogenous. Most Swiss simply use the most available local wine.

If you feel the wine you have is not sufficiently acidic, add a little lemon juice. A good rule of thumb is 1 tsp of lemon juice to each ½ cup (120 ml) of wine.

A reasonable rule for balancing wine against cheese is to use ½ cup (120 ml) wine to 8 oz (225 g) cheese. Cheese will absorb liquid differently depending upon its kind and age, so start with a little less wine and add more as needed.

**Additions:** Let your imagination go. Vary cheese fondues with the addition of sautéed celery, onions, leeks, sweet peppers, minced brown mushrooms, fennel, chervil, or sorrel. In fact, just about anything you can put in an omelette works in a cheese fondue.

## Culinary Cues

• Read the recipes and assemble all the ingredients before you start. The cooking moves very rapidly once you have begun.

• Remember that cheese fondues must cook over very LOW heat or they become stringy.

• Always keep the cheese hot, despite the low heat, so that it will not become tough.

• When the cheese fondue has achieved a smooth consistency, transfer it to the warming stand at once. Do not permit it to cool even a few degrees.

• When adding cheese to the wine, stir constantly but not in a clockwise or counterclockwise fashion; stir in the shape of a figure eight.

• If the cheese does not thicken at once, don't worry; just keep stirring.

• To make the fondue a little lighter, add a pinch of baking soda.

• Once the fondue is made, keep it bubbling.

• If the fondue becomes lumpy, or the liquid becomes separated from the solids, put the fondue back on the stove, whip it thoroughly with a wire whisk, and add ½ tsp of cornstarch. If only a small quantity of fondue remains, make a paste of the cornstarch with 2 oz (60 ml) of the wine or other liquid ingredient before adding it to the fondue.

• If the fondue turns lumpy despite your care in following instructions, it may well not be your fault. Cheese that has not matured properly tends to become lumpy and form "threads." This can be avoided by adding a little Gruyère to your Swiss cheese fondue; or if you are using both cheeses, adding a little more Gruyère.

• If the fondue becomes too thick due to continuous cooking and evaporation of the liquid, thin it by adding more liquid which has first been warmed—NEVER USE COLD LIQUID. To do this, put the fondue back on the stove, but be very careful to use just enough wine to maintain a creamy consistency. If the wine and thickened cheese do not blend, add ½ tsp cornstarch made into a paste with a little more wine.

• When serving a meat fondue, if the oil begins to cool at the table, return the oil to the stove and bring it to the boiling point again.

## Safety Hints

• Some recipes indicate that the oil in the fondue pot is ready when it "bubbles," but be aware that the oil might smoke—or even blaze—before it bubbles. It may appear to bubble when food is dipped into it. Cooking oil should be heated only until a small cube of fresh bread starts to brown—about 45 to 60 seconds. If the oil smokes, the pot should be removed at once from the heat.

• The fondue pot must sit on a secure, rimmed holder to reduce the chance of its sliding or being overturned at the table.

• The pot handle should always be turned away from the diners so that it cannot be struck by a hand or catch on a sleeve or cuff.

• Keep the pot away from the edge of the table—but not so far as to make it awkward to use.

• Do not use a ceramic pot for making any of the fondues except the cheese. Ceramic pots are not designed for the high temperatures required by noncheese fondues. For those, only use metal pots with sloping sides.

• The forks used to spear dunkables should be long enough so that the diners' hands will not be close to the pot's side or reach over its contents.

• Let the food cool for a moment before putting it in the mouth. Burned lips and tongue can spoil a meal more than burned food.

• To reduce spattering when cooking meat in oil, add 1 teaspoon of salt for every 3 cups (750 ml) of oil used. In addition, always blot the excess moisture from the meat cubes.

• If using an electric fondue pot, heat the oil about 15 minutes, or until it reaches 400°F (about 200°C).

• If you use a nonelectric fondue pot, heat the oil in an uncovered pan and watch it closely until it is ready.

• Never heat oil in a covered pan, since it may reach ignition and then flash into fire when uncovered.

• Never leave a cooking fondue unattended. And keep small children away from the table on which the fondue is being prepared.

## Eating Etiquette

• Each guest is armed with a fondue fork and, in turn, spears a piece of bread, makes a figure eight with it in the fondue, twirls the fork as it is lifted from the pot, and pops the cheese-coated bread into his or her mouth. A final dextrous swirl is necessary to keep the cheese on the bread; the swirling is much like gathering in spaghetti on a fork.

• Fondue is definitely not an occasion for the best table linen. A bright checkered cloth and napkins add to the gaiety.

• If you drop your bread in transit, tradition allows you to kiss your neighbor. A penalty variant is that you buy the next round of drinks.

• Toward the end of the meal, the cheese will form a brown crust on the bottom of the pot. This is justly considered a special treat (the luck of the pot) and is reserved for the person who has not dropped a piece of bread throughout the meal. The crust is easily lifted out with a fork.

• With a cheese fondue, only one person may dip at a time. With a meat fondue, several forks may rest in the pot, but in removing your fork be careful not to dislodge the meat from your neighbors' forks.

## Fondue Equipment

• The Swiss formerly made fondue in a heavy earthenware pot called a caquelon. Today, however, a copper pot is considered ideal because it holds the heat and distributes it evenly.

• When using a copper pot, a warmer is a necessary resting place for the pot after the fondue is ready to serve. Some people use an alcohol, Sterno, or candle warmer; others a small electric hot plate.

• Electrified fondue pots generally have thermostatically controlled temperature settings. Most have at least two settings: a LOW setting for heat-sensitive food such as cheese and a HIGH setting for dishes cooked in hot oil. The pots themselves are usually made of aluminum or stainless steel with a nonstick or ceramic interior.

• Long-handled, slender forks are needed to spear and put the dunkables into the fondue. Some sets come with color-coded handles so that the diners can keep track of their own. If you can't find fondue forks, metal skewers or even metal knitting needles might suffice.

• For meat fondues, regular forks are also required for eating; the cooking fork will be too hot to put into your mouth.

• You'll need plates to transfer the hot meats from the fondue fork to a table fork. These could have sections to hold a variety of sauces in for dipping the cooked food. Use separate plates for each guest's uncooked meat. This will help avoid bacteria and other microbes; do not eat anything from the uncooked plates.

• Finger bowls might be a good idea, half-filled with lukewarm water in which a slice of lemon is floated.

## Fond´oeuvre

The fondue in many of its variations makes a perfect hors d´oeuvre dish—whether for a cocktail party, a snack, or a first course.

You'll find a variety of recipes for fondues of all natures in this book—from cheese to meats to chocolate—that are readily adaptable as a conversation piece or the center of interest on the buffet table.

The recipes in the chapter "Monkeys and Rabbits" (pages 44–59) will serve equally well as hot cocktail dips and hors d´oeuvres.

## Cooking in Metric

When the first edition of this book, designed for North American cooks, was published in 1968, the metrics system was taught to math and science students, but rarely used in home economics courses.

In the late 20th century, however, many cookbooks have generic applications. Since metrics are used around the world, we hope to accommodate readers far and wide to help determine the proportions of recipe ingredients. You'll find a Metric Equivalents table on page 158. In the recipe ingredients lists, we've given metric equivalents in

parentheses. For tablespoons (Tbsp) and teaspoons (tsp), we leave it to you. The standard tablespoon is 15 ml and the standard teaspoon is 5 ml. Although we may suggest using, say, 1-inch (2.5-cm) dunkables, you don't have to worry about fine measurements; a 2-cm or 3-cm piece works just as well. The chunk of bread or other dunkable simply has to be big enough so that both fork prongs fit into it but not so big (or so small) that it will fall into the fondue pot.

Most of the recipes in this book suggest relative proportions of the necessary ingredients. Just as you adjust seasonings to individual taste in your everyday cooking (omitting the pepper or adding less than the required teaspoon), be aware that the mathematical equivalents given here may be subject to adjustment as well.

You can safely round up ½ cup to 125 ml or 1 cup to 250 ml instead of the usual 120 ml and 240 ml, if you wish. A recipe that calls for 4 cups of oil—into which you dip meat cubes for a beef fondue—may be equal to 960 ml, but you can safely and conveniently use a 1-liter bottle of oil. There is no need to carefully measure out 960 ml.

This also works for the quantities in a given can, jar, or package of prepared food, such as soup or anchovies. Just use a reasonable equivalent of the foodstuff, no matter what brand your local market carries. No, you don't have to be a mathematical genius.

## Using Prepared Foods

Some of the recipes in this book make use of commercially prepared foods—bottled, canned, or packaged in cartons and the like. You'll find recipes using vegetables (such as beans, corn, tomatoes) or fruit (cherries, peaches, pineapple), as well as soups, seafood, chili con carne, deviled ham, evaporated milk, bottled dressings, and more.

The can, bottle, or package quantity given in the recipe refers to what had been printed on the original product the author found in his hometown. We give the metric equivalent of the weight or volume to help you find the appropriate size in your local market.

## Choosing the Wine

Most recipes for cheese fondues that call for wine as an ingredient will specify a dry white wine. The traditional Swiss wine favored for fondues is Neuchâtel; today most Swiss prefer using a local wine that's very acidic. However, your choice of wine in the recipe may depend on whether you are making the fondue as an appetizer or a main dish. It may also depend on the wine's availability in your area. Neuchâtel may not be as readily available as Chablis, for instance.

In the wine list below, we've noted not only the type of wine (Sherry, Chablis, Rhine), but the characteristics (dry, pale, nutty) of the preferred wine, since some types include varieties with flavors or colors other than those most desirable for your fondue.

| Fondue's Use | Wine | Character of Wine |
|---|---|---|
| Appetizer | Sherry | Dry to very dry, pale amber, nutty flavor |
| Main Dish | Chablis | Very dry, pale gold, fresh, fruit flavor |
| | Chenin Blanc | Dry, well-balanced, rich, tart |
| | Moselle | Dry, pale, light-bodied |
| | Rhine | Dry, pale gold to slightly green-gold, light-bodied, tart |
| | Sauternes | Golden, full-bodied, fragrant |
| Appetizer or Main Dish | Champagne | Dry (brut, sec, demi-sec); pale gold; light-bodied, sparkling |
| | Neuchâtel | Dry, pale gold, light-bodied, lively, crisp |

## Dunkables

Normally for a Swiss fondue, or any variation on this cheese fondue, you'll need cubes of hard bread, about 1 inch (2 or 3 cm) square, to dunk into the mixture. Spear the bread on the fondue fork, dip it into the fondue pot, stir it around once or twice in a figure eight, and then devour the treat. If you use French or Italian bread, for four people you'll need one or two loaves, depending on the size of the loaf and the appetite of the guests. Cut cubes of bread with a crust on at least one side. Spear the cubes through the soft side and into the crust.

You can substitute a wide variety of edibles for the French or Italian bread, as imagination and taste allow. Here are a few suggestions. Make chunks or cubes of the vegetables or fruit so that you can easily spear them. You'll find Dessert Dunkables on pages 150–152.

Apple (tart)

Artichoke Hearts (halved)

Bagel, Focaccia, or Hard Rolls (onion, garlic, sesame, or "everything" chunks)

Broccoli Florets

Carrots

Cauliflower Florets

Celery

Cheese-Filled Small Ravioli

Cherry Tomatoes

Cucumber (thick slices)

Eggplant

Flour Tortillas (bite-size pieces)

Mushroom Caps

Pita, Nan, or Flat Breads (bite-size pieces)

Pepper Strips (green, red, or yellow)

Potatoes (new small, boiled, whole or halved)

Pumpernickel, Rye, or Whole Wheat Bread (chunks) or Toast (squares)

Radishes (whole or halved)

Sausages (tiny, grilled)

Yellow Squash

Zucchini

# A Swiss Classic

Emmenthaler isn't the only cheese to use.

*A* fondue is the kind of dish you serve to special people in your life. Basically, the fondue began as a cheese dish, cooked in wine and served with bread. As time went by, however, the fondue idea moved on and the melted cheese base was varied by the substitution of a number of other ingredients for it.

The cheese fondue appears on menus under a variety of names, such as Swiss Fondue or Fondue Neuchâteloise. The latter name derives from the fact that the dry white wine used is often from Neuchâtel, a Swiss canton on the French border. But when it comes to choosing a wine in which to melt the cheese, the choice is the cook's—just be sure that it provides the required acidity. As already noted, if you feel the wine's acidity is not sufficient, add lemon juice to compensate (see page 11).

Aside from Neuchâtel, some appropriate wines are Rhine, Sauternes, Chablis, or Moselle. The wines produced from the grapes grown in the chalky soil of the Auvernier, Boudry, and Colombier vineyards west of Neuchâtel are naturals for fondue, as is Fendant from the Valais.

Although many people consider kirsch as basic to an authentic fondue, some do not use it at all, and others substitute cognac, light rum, applejack, dry vermouth, or slivovitz.

An important point to remember about making a cheese fondue is that if the mixture starts to become too thick, it can be thinned with a little more wine, provided the wine has been preheated.

It isn't necessary to wash down the mildly alcoholic fondue with any beverage. Cold beer or cold water are out, however, because—many Swiss will tell you—they would upset the fondue eater's stomach. Instead, a glass of the same wine that went into the pot or perhaps a tumbler with two fingers of kirsch, that colorless liquid distilled from black cherries, is recommended.

After bread cubes have been dipped into cheese fondue, you can enjoy a tangy addition. Fill small bowls with such seeds as sesame, caraway, coriander, or fennel and place them around the table. They'll add an interesting taste. You'll find a whole range of interesting possibilities in the chapter "Sauces Sweet and Spicy" (pages 107–130).

# ❖ FONDUE SUISSE ❖

Makes 4 servings

*1 clove garlic*

*1 lb (450 g) Swiss cheese, finely diced*

*3 Tbsp flour*

*2 cups (480 ml) dry white wine*

*1 Tbsp lemon juice (if desired, see page 11)*

*½ cup (120 ml) kirsch*

*salt*

*¼ tsp white pepper*

*nutmeg* OR *paprika*

Cut garlic into halves, rub inside of a fondue pot until well flavored, and then discard garlic. Pour wine into the pot and place over LOW heat until bubbles start rising to the surface—DO NOT BOIL. Add lemon juice at this point if required.

Place cheese in a bowl, sprinkle with flour, and mix lightly. Then add the cheese mixture by handfuls, constantly stirring with a wooden fork or spoon in a figure-eight pattern until cheese is melted. Be sure each handful is melted before you add the next.

After the last of the cheese has been added and the mixture begins to bubble, quickly add kirsch and seasonings to taste, stirring until blended.

## SWISS FONDUE VARIATIONS

# FONDUE NEUCHÂTELOISE

This "double" fondue is as popular in Switzerland as the basic Swiss cheese version. By using two cheeses instead of one, you will find a distinctive flavor difference that is highly tangy.

Use the same ingredients as for Fondue Suisse, except that instead of using Swiss cheese, use a half-and-half mixture of Swiss and Gruyère. Follow the directions for Fondue Suisse.

# TRIPLE FONDUE

By adding a third cheese to the Neuchâteloise recipe, you have another tongue-titillating taste. Use equal amounts of each cheese—Gruyère, Gorgonzola, and Tilsit. Follow the directions for Fondue Suisse.

# CARAWAY FONDUE

This variation of Fondue Suisse calls for Swiss cheese and caraway-seed cheese. Use equal amounts of the two cheeses and follow the directions for Fondue Suisse.

# ADD-AN-EGG FONDUE

In this variation, the final ingredient (the egg) is added after you have consumed about two-thirds of the Fondue Suisse. At that point, add 1 or 2 large raw eggs. Stir vigorously with a fork. You may want to add a little salt for seasoning.

# MUSHROOM FONDUE

Use 4 oz (about 100 g) of chopped mushrooms for each 8 oz (225 g) Swiss cheese. Chop the mushrooms with a little minced onion, to taste. Sauté in hot butter until the vegetable liquid has evaporated. Add the sautéed mushrooms to the Fondue Suisse recipe when it is ready to be eaten.

# TRUFFLE FONDUE

Use 4 oz (110 g or about ½ cup) of chopped truffles for each 8 oz or (225 g ) Swiss cheese. Chop truffles finely. Sauté in a little hot butter. Add to the Fondue Suisse recipe when it is ready to be eaten.

# FONDUE À LA CHAMPAGNE

Instead of white wine, use a dry Champagne or sparkling wine.

# PINK FONDUE

Instead of white wine, use a very dry rosé.

# FONDUE FLAMBÉE

After the fondue (any of the above variations except "Fondue à la Champagne") is ready to be eaten, heat about ¼ cup (60 ml) kirsch—or more, to taste—in a ladle. Pour the hot liqueur over the bubbling fondue. Flame. When the flame has died down, it is ready to be eaten.

# TOMATO FONDUE

Peel and seed 2 tomatoes; then chop very fine. Add to the fondue when it is ready to be eaten.

## OTHER VARIATIONS

There are any number of other variations that depend upon the type of cheese you use—or, in fact, the combination of cheeses. This leaves your culinary talents open to your own taste in cheese and your palate as far as mixing cheeses.

In Switzerland, of course, the many local cheeses—and local wines—tend to give the fondues available a variety of flavors difficult to duplicate anywhere else in the world. But the same applies to wherever you live. Experiment with local cheeses, and with local wines. But remember, the wines should be dry—even if your own preference in drinking wine is to the sweeter side.

In the Valais district of Switzerland, the fondue makers use such local cheeses as Bagnes, Gomser, and Orsière, which sometimes show up in your local cheese specialty shop. If they do, and you decide to experiment, DO NOT USE WINE. Instead, use hot milk, preferably skim or 1% milk.

In Fribourg, the fondue is made with Vacherin cheese—but this is melted in hot water rather than in hot wine or hot milk. The Fribourg version does not use any kirsch. Another variation from the norm we know, which the Fribourgers use, is in the choice of dunkables—they use potato sections, usually partially boiled but sometimes raw.

# ❖ FONDUE GRUYÈRE ❖

Makes 4 to 6 servings

*1 clove garlic*

*2 lb (about 1 kg) Gruyère cheese*

*2 cups (480 ml) dry white wine*

*½ cup (120 ml) kirsch*

*1 tsp cornstarch*

*salt*

*white pepper*

Cut garlic into halves, rub inside of a fondue pot until well flavored, and then discard the garlic. Shred cheese into the pot. Pour wine over cheese. Place the pot over HIGH heat, stirring mixture slowly but constantly with a wooden spoon in a figure-eight pattern.

Dissolve the cornstarch in the kirsch. Add the cornstarch mixture to the cheese mixture, when the cheese begins to boil. Add salt and pepper to taste and stir until well blended.

Remove from HIGH heat to a warming stand, making sure the fondue keeps bubbling lightly.

# ❖ PUNGENT CHEESE FONDUE ❖

Makes 4 servings

*2 Tbsp butter* OR *margarine*

*3 Tbsp flour*

*2 cups (480 ml) milk*

*salt*

*paprika*

*nutmeg*

*1 lb (450 g) ripe domestic Cheddar cheese, finely diced*

Melt butter or margarine in a fondue pot. Add flour, stirring until smooth. Add milk very slowly, stirring constantly so that lumps do not form. Add salt to taste; make sure it is stirred in thoroughly. Add paprika and nutmeg to taste.

Cook for 3 to 4 minutes over LOW heat. Add cheese a bit at a time, making sure it melts before adding more. Remove from heat to a warming stand.

## PUNGENT CHEESE FONDUE VARIATIONS

For a different flavor combination, use either ripe Brie or Camembert. Remove any cheese rind that has turned green.

# ❖ FONDUE PORCINI ❖

Makes 6 servings (10 to 12 as an appetizer)

1 cup plus 2 Tbsp (270 ml) Marsala wine
¾ cup (180 ml) dried wild mushrooms
8 oz (225 g) grated Fontina cheese
8 oz (225 g) grated Swiss cheese
2 to 3 Tbsp (30–45 ml) all-purpose flour
1 clove garlic, halved
2 cups (480 ml) dry white wine
½ cup (120 ml) grated Parmesan OR Pecorino OR Romano cheese
freshly ground pepper

In a small pan, heat 1 cup (240 ml) of the Marsala just to the boiling point. Pour the heated wine over the mushrooms in a small bowl and let stand 1 hour.

Toss the Fontina and Swiss cheeses with the flour. Rub the fondue pot with the garlic; then pour the white wine into the pot and heat it over MEDIUM LOW heat until the wine is hot. Add the cheese and flour combination, a handful at a time, stirring constantly and waiting until each addition melts before adding the next. Stir in the Parmesan.

Drain the mushrooms, squeezing out as much liquid as possible. Then chop finely. Add the chopped mushrooms, the remaining Marsala, and the ground pepper (to taste). Stir well.

NOTE: Crusty bread cubes make an ideal dunkable. Also try slices of grilled Italian sausages. Serve with a chilled Italian white wine and a green salad. The chapter "The Other Side of the Dish" (pages 131–136) suggests other accompaniments.

# ❖ TWO-CHEESE FONDUE ❖

Makes 4 servings

*3 Tbsp butter* OR *margarine*
*3 Tbsp flour*
*cayenne pepper*
*¾ cup (180 ml) light cream*
*¾ cup (180 ml) chicken stock*
*1 tsp dried minced onion*
*4 oz (110 g) Parmesan cheese, shredded*
*4 oz (110 g) Swiss cheese, diced finely*

Melt butter or margarine in a fondue pot. Blend in flour and cayenne pepper to taste. Add liquids gradually. Add onion, stirring constantly until mixture thickens. Add cheese, cooking until melted. Remove from heat to a warming stand.

# ❖ FONDUE MONTEREY-MÜNSTER ❖

Makes 4 servings

*2 Tbsp butter*

*4 cloves garlic, minced*

*½ cup (120 ml) red onion, diced*

*5 tsp (25 ml) cornstarch*

*2 cups (480 ml) white wine, divided*

*1 tsp chili flakes*

*1 lb (450 g) Monterey Jack cheese, grated*

*1 lb (450 g) Münster cheese, grated*

*3 Tbsp fresh cilantro, chopped*

*1 small red pepper, finely diced*

*2 jalapeño peppers, seeded, diced*

Melt butter in a fondue pot over MEDIUM heat on a stove. Sauté the garlic and onions until they just begin to turn transparent; do not brown.

Mix the cornstarch with ¼ cup (60 ml) of wine. Add this mixture along with the remaining wine to the pot. Bring to a boil; then reduce heat to a simmer and add the chili flakes.

Add the cheese alternately by the handful, stirring to melt and being sure to meld each handful before adding the next. Make sure the mixture is well blended; DO NOT ALLOW TO BOIL. Stir in the cilantro and peppers just before serving. Remove from HIGH heat to a warming stand, making sure the fondue keeps bubbling lightly.

## SERVING SUGGESTION

Dunk tortilla chips, sweet pepper chunks, or chunks of French bread.

# ❖ FETA FONDUE ❖

Makes 6 servings

*1 cup (240 ml) milk*

*1 clove garlic, minced*

*8 oz (225 g) cream cheese*

*8 oz (225 g) feta cheese (soft, with rind)*

*1 Tbsp cornstarch*

*1 Tbsp chopped fresh rosemary*

*1 Tbsp chopped fresh thyme*

*2 Tbsp balsamic vinegar*

*½ tsp pepper*

*salt*

Mix milk and garlic in a saucepan over MEDIUM heat. Cut cream cheese into cubes; add to mixture, heating gently and stirring until melted, about 2 to 3 minutes.

Break or cut feta into small chunks, toss with cornstarch in a small bowl, and add to pot. Stir gently until melted. Stir in remaining ingredients and transfer to a fondue pot.

## SERVING SUGGESTION

Roasted potatoes, roasted peppers, artichoke hearts (raw or grilled), olives. Cubes of smoked chicken can be used in combination with the vegetable chunks, or you can use the chicken cubes alone, to make this an even more unusual taste treat.

# ❖ FONTINA ❖

Makes 4 servings

*2 Tbsp butter* OR *margarine*
*4 Tbsp (60 ml) flour*
*4 cups (960 ml) milk*
*1 lb (450 g) Swiss cheese, diced finely*
*¼ tsp salt*
*nutmeg*

Melt butter or margarine in a fondue pot. Add the flour and stir over MEDIUM heat until blended.

Add milk gradually. Add cheese by handfuls, stirring continuously until the cheese melts completely. Add salt and nutmeg to taste, stirring until smooth. Remove from heat to a warming stand.

# ❖ FONDUE PAISANO ❖

Makes 6 servings

*1 glove garlic*
*1 cup (240 ml) dry white wine*
*1 lb (450 g) Swiss cheese, diced*
*1½ tsp potato flour*
*cold water*
*1 tsp oregano*
*salt and pepper*
*2 Tbsp sherry*

Rub inside of fondue pot with the garlic. Pour in the white wine and bring to a simmer. Add cheese a little at a time, stirring with a wire whisk, until melted and well blended.

Mix potato flour with a little cold water, then blend into the cheese mixture. Season with the oregano and use salt and pepper to taste. Add the sherry.

# ❖ EGG FONDUE ❖

Makes 4 servings

*4 oz (110 g) butter* OR *margarine*

*3 Tbsp flour*

*½ tsp salt*

*½ tsp freshly ground pepper*

*2 to 2¼ cups (480–540 ml) milk*

*5 egg yolks, slightly beaten*

*¾ cup (180 ml) shredded Parmesan cheese*

Melt butter or margarine in a fondue pot over LOW heat. Add flour, stirring until frothy. Add salt, pepper and 2 cups (480 ml) of the milk all at once. Cook, stirring constantly until mixture thickens.

Pour a small amount of the resulting sauce into the egg yolks, stirring constantly. Pour egg mixture into sauce; cook, continuing to stir, for about 2 minutes or until thickened. DO NOT BOIL.

Add shredded cheese. If too thick, add more milk—but NOT MORE THAN ¼ cup (60 ml). Remove from heat to a warming stand.

# ❖ EGG FONDUE EMMENTHALER ❖

Makes 6 servings

*2 Tbsp butter*

*2 Tbsp flour*

*1 clove garlic, crushed*

*1 cup (240 ml) milk*

*1 cup (240 ml) Swiss cheese, finely shredded*

*3 large eggs, well beaten*

*½ cup (120 ml) dry white wine*

*salt and pepper*

Melt butter in a fondue pot over LOW heat. Stir in flour and garlic; cook for 2 minutes. Whisk in milk, stirring constantly until mixture is smooth and begins to thicken. Add cheese, stirring until smooth. Whisk eggs and wine together. Add salt and pepper to taste. Cook over LOW heat until mixture just begins to set but is still soft. Remove from heat to a warming stand.

# ❖ RED, YELLOW, AND BLUE ❖

Makes 6 servings

*1½ cups (360 ml) diced or shredded Cheddar cheese*

*½ cup (120 ml) crumbled blue cheese*

*1 tsp Worcestershire sauce*

*10-fl-oz (300-ml) can condensed tomato soup*

*2 Tbsp sherry*

Combine cheese, Worcestershire sauce, and soup in a fondue pot. Stir constantly over LOW heat until cheeses are melted and mixture is creamy. Add sherry and blend well. Remove from heat to a warming stand.

# ❖ CHILI CON QUESO ❖

Makes 6 to 8 servings

*2 onions*

*1 green pepper*

*4 oz (110 g) butter*

*8-oz (225-g) can kernel corn*

*1 lb (450 g) grated mild Cheddar*

*1 tsp chili powder*

*1 tsp salt*

*1 large egg, beaten*

*10-fl-oz (300-ml) can condensed tomato soup\**

Chop onions and pepper and cook in butter until soft. Add corn and cook 1 minute. Add cheese, chili powder, and salt (seasonings can be adjusted to taste). Blend beaten egg into soup and add to mixture. Cook, stirring constantly until thick and creamy.

\*If you prefer, you can use 4 large tomatoes, peeled and chopped, in place of the condensed soup. If you so choose, add the tomatoes with the onions and pepper, cooking them in butter until soft. Then stir in 1 Tbsp flour before adding the corn. Add the cheese and seasonings. Finally, add the beaten egg, blending it into the other ingredients. Cook, stirring constantly until thick and creamy.

### SERVING SUGGESTION

Mexican tortillas, squares of toasted bread, or both together, make ideal dunkables.

# ❖ CHILI VERDE CON QUESO ❖

Makes 4 to 6 servings

*1 large onion, chopped*

*2 Tbsp butter*

*19-fl-oz (570-ml) can tomatoes\*, drained and diced*

*4-fl-oz (120-ml) can green chilis, drained and chopped*

*8 oz (225 g) Monterey Jack cheese, diced*

*½ tsp marjoram*

*½ tsp salt*

In a skillet, sauté the onion in the butter. Add the remaining ingredients and cook over LOW heat until the cheese has melted. Transfer to a fondue pot for serving.

\*Note that there are many styles of canned tomatoes available—Mexican, Italian, Chili, etc.—providing subtle taste variances.

### SERVING SUGGESTION

Corn chips or tortilla chips make a tasty accompaniment to chunks of French bread.

# ❖ BEAN FONDUE ❖

### Serves 4 to 6

*16-fl-oz (480-ml) can pork and beans in tomato sauce*
*1 Tbsp butter*
*½ lb (225 g) lean ground chuck*
*3 Tbsp onion, finely chopped*
*½ cup (120 ml) mild Cheddar, shredded*
*1 tsp garlic powder*
*1 tsp lemon juice*
*1 tsp horseradish-style mustard*
*3 drops Tabasco sauce*

Put beans in a food blender and pulverize until they are finely puréed (or force them through a fine sieve); then set aside. Melt the butter in a fondue pot over MODERATE heat; add the ground chuck and sauté until it breaks apart and begins to brown slightly. Add the chopped onion and continue to sauté until the onion is limp and transparent.

Turn the heat to LOW and add the beans to the sautéed meat mixture. Mix thoroughly, stirring constantly, and cook until steaming hot. Add the Cheddar, continuing to stir until the cheese has completely melted. Add the garlic powder, lemon juice, mustard, and Tabasco sauce. Continue to cook and stir for a few minutes before serving.

### SERVING SUGGESTION

French bread, cornbread, and Italian bread chunks and tortilla chips or pieces of taco shells go well with this fondue.

# ❖ BEER AND CHEESE FONDUE ❖

Makes 4 servings

3 Tbsp cornstarch

¼ tsp dry mustard

1 can beer, divided

1 Tbsp caraway seeds

1 tsp Worcestershire sauce

½ clove garlic, crushed

8 oz (225 g) processed caraway-seed cheese

2 12-oz (335-g) packages frozen, fried, and
    breaded shrimps OR scallops

Combine cornstarch and mustard and stir in ¼ cup (60 ml) beer to make a smooth paste. Gradually stir in remaining beer. Add caraway seeds, Worcestershire sauce, and garlic. Stir constantly over MEDIUM heat until the mixture thickens and comes to a boil. Then reduce heat and simmer for 10 minutes.

Cut cheese into thin strips and add to mixture about one-third at a time, stirring after each addition until melted. Reset to keep mixture warm. Meanwhile, heat the frozen breaded shrimp or scallops as directed on the package label and use them as dunkables.

# ❖ FONDUE AU JUS DU RAISINS ❖

Makes 6 servings

*2 cups (480 ml) white grape juice, divided*

*1 garlic clove*

*1 lb (450 g) aged Swiss cheese, shredded*

*3 Tbsp cornstarch*

*¾ tsp salt*

*½ tsp Worcestershire sauce*

*¼ tsp white pepper*

*¼ tsp freshly grated nutmeg*

Heat 1¾ cups (420 ml) of the grape juice with the garlic in the top of a double boiler until very hot (placing this top saucepan directly on the burner). Then place the top pot over water in the lower pot and bring the water to a boil. Remove the garlic.

Add cheese, stirring constantly until it is all melted. (The cheese may not appear to thoroughly combine with the grape juice yet. The two ingredients will be completely combined after the next step.)

Combine cornstarch, salt, Worcestershire sauce, pepper, and nutmeg with the remaining grape juice and stir into the cheese mixture. (The cheese will begin to combine with the grape juice after the cornstarch is introduced.) Continue heating until the mixture is smooth.

## ❖ ONION CHEESE FONDUE ❖

Makes 6 servings

*1 envelope onion soup mix*

*2 cups (480 ml) tomato juice*

*4 tsp (20 ml) lemon juice*

*1 lb (450 g) Cheddar cheese, shredded*

Combine onion soup mix and the tomato and lemon juices in a fondue pot. Heat slowly; when the mixture begins to simmer, add cheese by handfuls, stirring after each handful until the cheese melts. Remove from heat to a warming stand.

## ❖ QUICKIE FONDUE I ❖

Makes 3 or 4 servings

*¾ cup (180 ml) dry white wine*

*1 package cheese sauce mix*

*1 cup (240 ml) Swiss cheese, grated*

Slowly stir wine into the cheese sauce mix. Add cheese and cook over LOW heat, stirring until the mixture comes to a boil and thickens.

# ❖ QUICKIE FONDUE II ❖

Makes 4 to 6 servings

*10-fl-oz (300-ml) can condensed Cheddar cheese soup*
*½ cup (120 ml) Swiss cheese, cubed*
*1 medium garlic clove*

Heat soup, cheese, and garlic until cheese is melted, stirring occasionally. Remove garlic clove and serve.

# ❖ OUT-OF-A-CAN FONDUE ❖

Makes 2 servings

*1 clove garlic*
*dry white wine*
*1 can Swiss Fondue\**
*nutmeg*
*white pepper*
*2 to 3 Tbsp (30–45 ml) kirsch*

Cut garlic into halves, rub it inside a fondue pot until well flavored, and then discard garlic. Cover the bottom of a pot about ¼ inch (0.5 cm) deep in wine. Heat, but DO NOT BOIL. Stir canned fondue slowly into the hot wine; season to taste with nutmeg and pepper. Stir in kirsch just before serving. Remove from heat to a warming stand.

\*Some excellent, and authentic, Swiss fondue is available already prepared in cans. Just add a little extra kirsch and seasoning.

# *Monkeys and Rabbits*

A Welsh predecessor to fondues?

*ust as there is dispute over the origin of the word* fondue, *so there is controversy over the word* rabbit—*or* rarebit, *as some prefer to spell it (and some to pronounce it).*

*Some claim that Welsh Rabbit derived from a situation in which a Welsh chieftain once found himself. His larder was out of game, it is related, and unexpected guests were served toasted cheese on bread. The glib chieftain is said to have told his friends that the dish they were being served was "a Welsh rabbit."*

*Others insist that the spelling and pronunciation are both* rarebit, *derived from the fact that the dish is "a rare bit of gastronomical pleasure." And it is! However, when you're the cook, you may call it whatever you like.*

*Exponents of the rabbit claim that it predates the Swiss fondue. They say that the fondue is only a Swiss version of the Welsh dish, but lovers of cheese cookery agree that both could rightly be called a Cheese Dream.*

*The rabbit is made essentially in the same way as the fondue, except that the cheese is Cheddar and the liquid is often milk and sometimes beer.*

# ❖ CLASSIC WELSH RABBIT ❖

Makes 4 servings

*2 Tbsp butter* OR *margarine*

*2 Tbsp flour*

*1 Tbsp dry mustard*

*1 cup (240 ml) milk*

*1 Tbsp Worcestershire sauce*

*cayenne pepper*

*8 oz (225 g) Cheddar cheese, shredded or broken into small pieces**

*3 Tbsp beer*

*toast* OR *toasted English muffins*

Melt butter or margarine in top of a double boiler over boiling water. Add flour and dry mustard and mix well. Add milk gradually, stirring until mixture thickens. Add Worcestershire sauce and a pinch of cayenne pepper to taste.

Add cheese and stir until cheese is melted. Stir in beer and serve at once over toast or English muffins.

* If process Cheddar is used, the dish can be made ahead of time and reheated. If regular Cheddar is used, it can be prepared slightly ahead of time with the cheese and beer added just before serving. (Regular Cheddar will become rubbery if allowed to stand too long.)

## RABBIT VARIATIONS

To add variety to a rabbit dish, forgo the toast or English muffins and serve it over one of these edibles.

*Asparagus Spears on sliced ham*

*Broccoli or Cauliflower Florets on sliced ham*

*Bacon (crisped side or back rashers)*

*Chicken (slices of cooked breast)*

*Chinese Pea Pods*

*Crabmeat, Lobster, or Shrimp (cooked bits on rice)*

*Deviled Ham on toast*

*Eggs (hard-boiled and sliced)*

*Kidney or Navy Beans*

*Mushrooms*

*Poached Eggs on toast*

*Sardines*

*String Beans*

*Tomato slices sprinkled with salt, pepper, and chopped onion, and then broiled*

*Tongue slices*

# ❖ YORKSHIRE BUCK ❖

Makes 4 servings

1 lb (450 g) sharp Cheddar cheese, shredded
2 Tbsp heavy cream
½ to ¾ cup (120–180 ml) stale beer OR ale
½ tsp salt
½ tsp freshly grated nutmeg
1 tsp Worcestershire sauce
pepper
2 large eggs, lightly beaten
4 large poached eggs on toast

Combine cheese, cream, and beer or ale in a heavy saucepan or fondue pot. Cook over LOW heat, stirring constantly until cheese is melted.

Add salt, nutmeg, and Worcestershire sauce; add a pinch of pepper to taste. Reduce heat and stir in beaten eggs, whisking constantly with a wire whisk until mixture is thickened and creamy. Spoon over poached eggs on toast.

# ❖ CHESHIRE RABBIT ❖

Makes 4 servings

*4 Tbsp (60 ml) butter*
*4 slices bread, toasted*
*beer* OR *ale*
*4 slices sharp Cheddar cheese*
*4 slices white Cheshire cheese*
*4 slices young Lancashire cheese*
*dry mustard*

Preheat oven to 400°F (200°C). Place 1 Tbsp of butter in each of four individual baking dishes or ramekins and set them in the oven until the butter is melted.

Place a slice of toast in each dish and moisten with a little beer or ale. Lay 1 slice of each of the 3 cheeses over each piece of moistened toast. Sprinkle with dry mustard to taste.

Put baking dishes in the oven for about 15 minutes, or until cheese is completely melted. Serve immediately.

## NOTE

A similar combination may be made of other cheeses, using one sharp cheese, one bland cheese, and one of a softer, younger type.

# ❖ BEER RABBIT ❖

Makes 6 servings

¼ *tsp paprika*

½ *tsp dry mustard*

*cayenne pepper*

⅔ *cup (160 ml) beer* OR *ale*

*1½ to 2 tsp (7.5–10 ml) Worcestershire sauce*

*1 lb (450 g) process sharp Cheddar cheese, shredded*

*toast* OR *alternatives*

In a skillet, mix paprika, mustard, and a dash or two of cayenne pepper to taste. Stir in beer or ale and Worcestershire sauce. Place over LOW heat; when beer is hot, add cheese and stir constantly until the cheese is completely melted.

Serve over toast, crackers, or your choice of accompaniments (see page 46).

## BEER RABBIT VARIATION

Use light or heavy cream instead of beer. The same quantity will be required.

# ❖ SHIRLEY TEMPLE RABBIT ❖

Makes 2 servings

*2 Tbsp butter*

*1 tsp Worcestershire sauce*

*½ tsp salt*

*½ tsp paprika*

*¼ tsp prepared mustard*

*½ lb (225 g) Cheddar cheese, shredded*

*½ cup (120 ml) ginger ale*

*1 large egg, slightly beaten*

*raisin bread, toasted*

Melt butter in top of a double boiler over boiling water. Add the Worcestershire sauce, salt, paprika, prepared mustard, and Cheddar cheese. Stir until the cheese melts. Add the ginger ale and egg; cook until thick.

Serve on toasted raisin bread.

# ❖ RABBIT CREOLE ❖

Makes 4 servings

*2 Tbsp butter*

*½ small onion, grated,* OR *½ tsp onion powder*

*1 green pepper, chopped*

*½ cup (120 ml) chopped ripe olives*

*1 tsp Creole seasoning* OR *Tabasco sauce*

*1 cup (240 ml) fresh peeled tomatoes* OR *drained canned tomatoes*

*1 cup (240 ml) Cheddar cheese, broken into small pieces*

*2 large eggs*

*rye bread, toasted*

Melt the butter slowly in a fondue pot. Add onion or onion powder, green pepper, olives, seasoning, and tomatoes. Simmer until the tomatoes and onion are soft (about 10 minutes).

Add cheese, stirring constantly over LOW heat (or over boiling water if not using a fondue pot) until the cheese melts. Beat eggs well, add and stir until mixture is creamy.

Serve over rye toast.

## NOTE

This recipe can be made in a double boiler, setting the top part directly on the heat source for the first part of the recipe. Or you can make it in a saucepan which is set in a pan of hot water when you add the eggs. Making it in a fondue pot is best, however, since you can serve it in the same pot.

# ❖ CHEESE AND TOMATO MONKEY ❖

Makes 4 servings

*1 cup (240 ml) Cheddar cheese, broken into small pieces*

*1 cup (240 ml) canned tomatoes, drained*

*½ cup (120 ml) soft bread crumbs*

*¼ tsp salt*

*pepper*

*½ tsp Creole seasoning OR Tabasco sauce*

*hard-boiled eggs, sliced, OR another nonbread base*

Combine all ingredients except the eggs in top of a double boiler. Stir over LOW heat until the cheese is melted. Serve over sliced hard-boiled eggs or another nonbread base of your choice.

# ❖ FONDUE POMODORO ❖

Makes 3 to 4 servings

8 *medium tomatoes*

4 *Tbsp butter*

½ *tsp salt*

1 *tsp sugar*

½ *tsp grated nutmeg*

*basil*

8 *oz (225 g) natural Gruyère cheese, shredded*

1 *large egg, beaten*

*toast*

Scald tomatoes and slip off skins. Cut tomatoes into halves when they are cool; gently squeeze out the seeds and excess juice. Chop the tomatoes finely, place them in a fondue pot, and sauté gently in butter. When the tomatoes are soft, add salt, sugar, and nutmeg as well as a pinch or two of basil to taste.

Add cheese a handful at a time, stirring until melted. Stir in the beaten egg just before serving, being sure to stir quickly and beat hard to prevent the egg white from coagulating.

Serve on toast.

# ❖ TOMATO SWISS FONDUE ❖

Makes 4 to 6 servings

*2 cups (480 ml) tomato juice, divided*

*1 clove of garlic*

*1 lb (450 g) aged Swiss cheese, shredded*

*3 Tbsp cornstarch*

*¾ tsp salt*

*½ tsp Worcestershire sauce*

*½ tsp crushed basil leaves*

*¼ tsp white pepper*

*¼ tsp freshly grated nutmeg*

Heat 1¾ cups (420 ml) tomato juice with the garlic clove in the top of a double boiler until very hot. Place over boiling water.

Remove the garlic clove; add cheese a small amount at a time, stirring constantly until the cheese is melted. (The cheese and tomato juice may not yet be thoroughly combined—see next step.)

Combine cornstarch, salt, Worcestershire sauce, basil, pepper, and nutmeg with the remaining ¼ cup (60 ml) of tomato juice. Stir this tomato juice mixture into the cheese mixture. Continue beating until the blend becomes completely smooth. Transfer to a fondue pot and serve.

# ❖ CHEESE DITTY ❖

Makes 4 servings

*8 oz (225 g) process Cheddar cheese, shredded*
*10-fl-oz (300-ml) can condensed tomato soup*
*1 Tbsp minced onion*
*1 Tbsp ketchup*
*¾ tsp dry mustard*
*salt*
*pepper*
*1 large egg, beaten*
*toast OR rusks*

Melt cheese in top of a double boiler over boiling water.

Combine the onion, ketchup, mustard, salt, and pepper to taste. Add to the soup and heat in a separate pot, and add the entire mixture to the cheese, stirring well. Add beaten egg gradually, stirring constantly. Cook for 5 minutes, stirring throughout.

Serve on toast or rusks.

# ❖ CHEESE CHILLALY ❖

Makes 4 to 6 servings

*1 Tbsp butter*

*2 Tbsp chopped green pepper*

*1 Tbsp chopped onion*

*½ cup (120 ml) canned tomatoes, drained*

*12 oz (335 g) soft milk cheese, finely diced*

*½ tsp salt*

*cayenne pepper*

*2 Tbsp milk*

*1 large egg, slightly beaten*

*crackers, toast OR English muffins*

Melt butter in a saucepan. Add green pepper and onion; cook slowly for 3 minutes. Add tomatoes; cook for 5 minutes. Add cheese, salt, and a few grains of cayenne pepper; cook slowly—or over hot water—until cheese melts. Stir in the milk and egg.

Serve immediately over a base of your choice.

# ❖ RUM TUM TIDDY ❖

Makes 4 servings

*10-fl-oz (300-ml) can condensed tomato soup*
*8 oz (225 g) quick-melting process cheese (such as Velveeta), shredded*
*½ tsp dry mustard*
*toast*

Combine all ingredients except toast and heat in a saucepan. Stir constantly until the cheese is melted. Serve over toast.

## THREE RUM-TUM-TIDDY VARIATIONS

**1.** Crumble crisp side bacon over the top of each serving; allow 1 slice of bacon per serving.

**2.** Add 1 cup (240 ml) cooked rice to the ingredients.

**3.** Add 7-oz (200-g) can drained whole-kernel corn to ingredients.

# ❖ FONDUE AU BRILLAT-SAVARIN ❖

### Makes 4 to 6 servings

*12 large eggs*

*8 oz (225 g) natural Gruyère cheese, shredded*

*4 oz (110 g) butter, softened*

*pepper, freshly ground*

*French bread cut in 1-inch (2.5-cm) slices, lightly toasted*

Beat eggs until frothy in a fondue pot. Add cheese and butter and place pot over very LOW heat (preferably above hot water in a lower pot). Stir mixture constantly until smooth and thickened. Stop stirring ONLY to grind pepper over the mixture.

Serve over toasted bread when the mixture is creamy.

# ❖ FONDUE VITE ❖

Makes 4 servings

*5.6-fl-oz (160-ml) can evaporated milk*

*½ lb (225 g) sharp cheese, cut into small pieces*

*¼ tsp dry mustard OR prepared mustard, to taste*

*1 large egg, slightly beaten*

*salt*

*white pepper*

*crackers OR toast*

Combine the milk and cheese in a fondue pot (or in the top of a double boiler). Stir over LOW heat until the cheese is melted. Remove from heat, stir in mustard, egg, and salt and pepper to taste. Mix thoroughly.

Serve on crackers or toast.

# From France and Asia

Red meats make a delicious fondue.

*Now we come to a different category of fondues—the meat type, of which there are several interesting varieties. Meat fondues should be accompanied by a tossed salad, rösti potatoes (pages 131–136), and if desired, a Burgundy or your favorite red wine.*

*You will see that the recipe for Fondue au Boeuf (page 62) suggests that you may want to use clarified butter instead of cooking oil. If you prefer this, you'll find how to clarify butter on page 63.*

*Using clarified butter or cooking oil presents a potential hazard that one doesn't face with melted cheese. Oil that becomes overheated can suddenly—and startlingly—flare up. And the use of an improper dish can cause a searing spillage of hot and sticky contents.*

*Cooking oil should be heated only until a 1-inch (2.5 cm) cube of fresh bread browns in 45 to 60 seconds. If the oil begins to smoke, it is too hot and should be removed at once from the heat source.*

*Make sure that your fondue pot sits on a secure, rimmed holder to reduce the chance of its sliding or being overturned at the table. Keep the pot away from the edge of the table, but not too far as to make it awkward to use. Always turn the pot handle away from diners so that it cannot be struck by a hand or caught on a sleeve or cuff.*

Do not use a ceramic pot for meat fondues; use only metal pots with sloping sides. The forks should be long enough so that hands will not have to be held over the side of the hot pot. Transfer the food to a table fork before eating, so that you don't burn your mouth.

To reduce spattering when cooking meat in oil, place a small piece of bread in the bottom of the pot, or add 1 tsp salt for every 3 cups oil used. It also helps to blot excess moisture from the meat before cooking. If you are using an electric fondue pot, heat the oil about 15 minutes or until it reaches 400°F (200°C). If you use a nonelectric pot, heat the oil in an uncovered pan and watch it closely until ready. Never heat oil in a covered pan, because it can reach ignition point and then flash into fire when uncovered. Also review Safety Hints (page 13).

## Serving Suggestions

Meat fondues go well with a crisp tossed salad, without dressing, although a lemon-juice dressing may be used to contrast with the flavor of the cooking oil.

Rösti potatoes (find recipes in the chapter "The Other Side of the Dish," pages 131–136), make an ideal side dish, although potato chips can be a good substitute.

A Burgundy is an ideal wine with a meat fondue, although you may prefer your own favorite red wine. If you are a white wine drinker, keep it as dry as possible so as not to interfere with the flavor of the meat.

Choose from a variety of sauces from the chapter "Sauces Sweet and Spicy" (pages 107–130) to delight your palate.

## ❖ BEEF POMODORO ❖

Makes 4 to 6 servings (10 to 12 as an appetizer)

*1½ lb (675 g) beef tenderloin*

*14-fl-oz (420-ml) can tomato sauce*

*1 Tbsp vinegar*

*2 tsp sugar*

*1 tsp prepared horseradish*

*½ garlic clove, crushed*

Cut beef into 1-inch (2.5-cm) cubes. Combine tomato sauce, vinegar, sugar, horseradish, and crushed garlic. Spear cubes on fondue forks and cook to personal liking. Dip in tomato sauce mixture.

## ❖ FONDUE AU BOEUF ❖

*½ lb (225 g) lean sirloin per person*

*salad oil, peanut oil,* OR *clarified butter*

*sauces*

Cut the meat into cubes about ¾ to 1 inch (2–2.5 cm) each. Fill a fondue pot with oil or clarified butter (page 63) to the halfway mark and heat to the required temperature (page 61). Then set the pot over a warming unit on the serving table. Put a small piece of bread in the bottom of the pot to prevent spattering.

Spear one cube of meat at a time on a fondue fork and set it into the hot oil, cooking to individual taste. When it is done, transfer the meat from the fondue fork to a table fork, then dip it into the sauce of choice. Find sauces in the chapter "Sauces Sweet and Spicy" (pages 107–130).

## MEAT VARIATIONS

# PORK, VEAL, OR LAMB FONDUE

Use pork fillet, veal tenderloin, or leg of lamb instead of beef.

# VIANDE TRIPLEHEADER

Use a combination of beef, pork, and veal.

## OTHER VARIATIONS

Before cooking the meat, lightly season with salt and pepper. Or cook in a mixture of half peanut oil and half clarified butter.

> ### *How to Clarify Butter*
> Melt sweet butter over low heat or in the top of a double boiler over boiling water. When completely melted, remove from heat and allow milk solids to settle at the bottom. Strain into a jar through a fine sieve or cheesecloth.
>
> The jar should be kept tightly sealed in the refrigerator until you are ready to use the clarified butter. It may be kept this way for about 3 weeks.

# ❖ SWEET AND SOUR PORK FONDUE ❖

Makes 6 to 8 servings

*1¾ lb (785 g) roasted pork shoulder*

*1 hot red pepper*

*2 green bell peppers*

*3 Tbsp cornstarch*

*1 cup (240 ml) wine vinegar*

*1 cup (240 ml) firmly packed brown sugar*

*1 Tbsp sharp prepared mustard*

*1 Tbsp Worcestershire sauce*

*19-oz (530-g) can pineapple chunks with juice*

Cut the roasted pork into finger-thick strips. Seed the red pepper and chop finely. Core, seed, and dice the green peppers, and set the peppers aside.

Mix the cornstarch with the wine vinegar; add the sugar and cook until thick and clear. Then add the diced green and red peppers, spices, and pineapple chunks and juice. Cover and simmer for 10 minutes; place on a burner.

## SERVING SUGGESTIONS

Cooked rice, ladled into small bowls for each diner, makes an ideal accompaniment. A spoonful of the broth, with peppers and pineapple, can be poured over each serving of rice.

# ❖ CZAR'S FONDUE ❖

Makes 4 servings

*1 lb (450 g) boneless lamb steak* OR *leg of lamb*
*8-fl-oz (250-ml) bottle Russian dressing*
*4 cups (960 ml) salad oil*

Trim fat and cut lamb into 1-inch (2.5-cm) cubes. In a small bowl, toss lamb cubes with Russian dressing until well coated. Refrigerate 4 hours.

When ready to serve, drain lamb well. Heat salad oil to 425°F (220°C). Cubes should be allowed to cook about 1 minute.

## SERVING SUGGESTION

Use with Horseradish Dip (page 115), Horseradish and Mayonnaise (page 115), or Pink Horseradish Sauce (page 119).

# FRANKFURTER FONDUE

Cut regular franks into bite-size pieces. Or use whole cocktail wieners, Vienna sausages, or other small ready-to-eat (precooked) whole sausages. Cook briefly until browned and heated through.

# ❖ MIXED GRILL FONDUE ❖

Makes 4 to 6 servings

*1 lb (450 g) chicken breasts, slightly frozen*

*1 lb (450 g) filet mignon, slightly frozen*

*½ lb (225 g) lamb kidneys*

*2 green peppers*

*4 oz (110 g) bacon*

*1 clove garlic*

*1 cup (240 ml) salad oil*

*8 oz (225 g) butter* OR *margarine*

Bone and skin chicken; slice chicken and beef into 1-inch (2.5-cm) cubes. Remove fat and hard cores from kidneys and slice thinly. Clean and remove seeds from peppers and cut into 1-inch (2.5-cm) squares. Cook bacon until crisp; drain and crumble.

Rub the fondue pot with garlic, then heat the oil and butter over a MEDIUM flame to bubbling but not foaming.

## SERVING SUGGESTION

Diners spear a piece of the chicken, beef, kidney, or pepper and cook it to taste (about 1 minute).

Choose three or four of these sauces: Pink Horseradish Sauce (page. 119), Horseradish Dip (page 115), Horseradish and Mayonnaise Sauce (page 115), Sauce Diable (page 120), Mustard and Sour Cream Sauce (page 118), Hot Paprika Sauce (page 116), or Tartar-Relish Sauce (page 127).

# ❖ HAM CROQUETTES ❖

Makes 4 to 6 servings (10 to 12 as an appetizer)

1½ cups (360 ml) finely chopped cooked ham
¼ cup (60 ml) chopped green pepper
1 tsp prepared spicy mustard
¼ tsp salt
⅛ tsp pepper
hot pepper seasoning
1 large egg
flour
cornflake crumbs OR packaged dry bread crumbs
4 cups (960 ml) salad oil

Mix thoroughly the chopped ham, green pepper, mustard, salt, pepper, and a few drops of pepper seasoning to taste. Shape the mixture into balls, using a teaspoonful as your measuring guide. Beat the egg until foamy, in a pie plate. Roll each ham ball in flour until completely coated; dip in the beaten egg and then roll in crumbs. Refrigerate for at least 4 hours until firm and set.

When ready to serve, heat salad oil to 425°F (220°C).

### SERVING SUGGESTION

Use Sauce Diable (page 120), Sauce Tartare De Luxe (page 122), or Tartar-Relish Sauce (page 127).

# ❖ FONDUE AU DIABLE ❖

Makes 2 servings

*1 package cheese sauce mix*
*1 cup (240 ml) milk*
*4½-oz (125-g) can deviled ham*

Combine the cheese sauce mix and milk. Heat according to directions on the package. Add deviled ham, heat for several minutes, stirring occasionally.

### SERVING SUGGESTION

Bread chunks are probably the best dunkable for this dish.

# ❖ FONDUE CHILI ❖

Makes 4 to 6 servings

*15-oz (420-g) can chili con carne*
*14-fl-oz (420-ml) can tomato sauce*
*1 Tbsp cornstarch*
*8-oz (225-g) package shredded Cheddar cheese*

Heat chili to boiling. Mix tomato sauce with cornstarch, add to the chili, and stir until the mixture is boiling again. Add cheese; stir until cheese melts and the mixture thickens.

# ❖ FONDUE BACCHUS ❖

### Makes 4 to 6 servings

*1 package onion soup mix*

*3 cups (750 ml) water*

*1 cup (240 ml) dry red wine*

*6 whole peppercorns*

*½ tsp celery salt*

*4 sprigs parsley*

*1 bay leaf*

*2 lb (900 g) lean beef stewing meat*

*unseasoned meat tenderizer*

Blend onion soup mix, water, and wine and bring to a boil.

Crush the peppercorns. Mix the peppercorns, celery salt, parsley, and bay leaf; add this dry mixture to the liquid.

Boil until the liquid is reduced by half. Strain broth through a fine sieve and pour into a fondue pot. Before cubing the beef, thoroughly moisten all surfaces with water. Then sprinkle the tenderizer evenly. Pierce the meat deeply with a cooking fork at approximately ½-inch (1.25-cm) intervals. Cube the beef for individual dipping in broth until desired doneness.

# ❖ RABBIT FONDUE ❖

Makes 6 to 8 servings

*water*
*4 lb (1.8–2 kg) rabbit*
*seasoned instant meat tenderizer*
*2 cups (480–500 ml) vegetable oil for cooking*

Thoroughly moisten ready-to-cook, boned rabbit with water. Sprinkle tenderizer evenly over entire surface. (Note: Do not use salt in the preparation of this dish.) Pierce meat deeply and thoroughly with a kitchen fork. Cut meat into 1½-inch (3.75-cm) cubes.

Make sure the oil is hot and ready to cook the meat to a well-done state (about 5 to 7 minutes) immediately upon cubing the rabbit.

# ❖ RABBIT FONDUE SAUCE ❖

*1 small onion, finely chopped*
*1 Tbsp vegetable oil*
*3 Tbsp chili sauce*
*½ cup (120 ml) dry white wine*
*½ cup (120 ml) sliced ripe olives*
*2-oz (55-g) can mushroom stems and pieces*
*1½ cups (360 ml) sour cream*

Brown the onion in oil. Add chili sauce, wine, olives, and mushrooms. Simmer about 20 minutes. Blend in sour cream just before serving.

VARIATION: Omit the chili sauce and olives and replace with ¼ cup (60 ml) cranberry jelly.

# ❖ SLOPPY JOE FONDUE ❖

Makes 3 to 4 servings

*1 lb (450 g) lean ground beef*
*½ cup (120 ml) onion, finely chopped*
*14-fl-oz (420-ml) can tomato sauce*
*¼ cup (60 ml) crisp sautéed bacon, finely crushed*
*4 oz (110 g) grated American cheese*
*¼ tsp salt*
*⅛ tsp freshly ground pepper*
*dash nutmeg*

Place the beef in a fondue pot over MODERATE heat and sauté until it loses its reddish color and begins to break apart. Add the onion; continue to sauté until the onion is limp and transparent. Pour off excess grease. Add tomato sauce and bacon, and continue to cook until the mixture begins to bubble—about 5 minutes.

Reduce heat to LOW and gradually add the cheese a little at a time, stirring each time until the cheese has melted. Add salt, pepper, and nutmeg. Mix well.

## SERVING SUGGESTIONS

You can serve this fondue mixture in the traditional Sloppy Joe manner, ladling it over hamburger buns.

Rye rolls, cut into bite-size pieces, make an interesting dunkable.

FABULOUS FONDUES

# ❖ QUICK SLOPPY JOE ❖

Makes 3 to 4 servings

*15¼-oz (458-ml) can prepared Sloppy Joe Mix*

*1 Tbsp onion, finely chopped*

*½ tsp oregano*

*½ tsp fennel seed*

*4 oz (110 g) shredded American cheese*

Put the prepared mix in a fondue pot over LOW heat until the mixture is warmed through and begins to bubble slightly. Add the onion, oregano, and fennel, stirring frequently for about 5 minutes. Gradually add the cheese, stirring continuously, until all the cheese has melted.

Serve like Sloppy Joe Fondue (page 71).

# ❖ FONDUE ORIENTALE ❖

Makes 3 to 4 servings

*½ lb (225 g) per person a variety of meats: beef (rump OR top round), lean veal, pork fillet OR tenderloin, lamb, veal kidneys, lamb kidneys, calves' liver, sweetbreads, chicken, OR fish fillets*

*beef OR chicken bouillon*

*sauces (pages 107–130)*

Slice all meats wafer thin or cut them into bite-size pieces if you prefer. Your butcher can slice them for you. But if you slice them at home, the job will be easier if you freeze the meats slightly beforehand.

Fill the pot two-thirds full with bouillon and bring to a boil. The bouillon MUST continue to boil throughout the meal. Spear one or more meats at the same time on the fondue fork and dip it into the bouillon, cooking to individual taste.

Remember: Pork should be cooked sufficiently, and kidneys get tough if cooked too long.

Transfer to table fork and dip in the sauce of choice.

## NOTE

If you use kidneys, they must be soaked in cold water for half an hour before slicing. The water should be changed three times. Then drain and dry the kidneys, and remove ALL fat and hard cores.

## ❖ FONDUE CHINOISE ❖

*½ lb (225 g) per person thinly sliced beef*
*beef bouillon*
*sauces, featuring soy sauce*

Prepare in the same fashion as Fondue Orientale (page 73).

## ❖ FONDUE JAPONAISE ❖

Makes 3 to 4 servings

*½ lb (225 g) sirloin* OR *round steak*
*½ small Chinese cabbage*
*4 green onions*
*2 small carrots*
*4 oz (110 g) small mushrooms*
*5 cups (1.25 L) chicken stock*

Freeze the steak for 20 minutes to make slicing easier. Cut cabbage into small pieces. Cut onions into 2-inch (5-cm) lengths. Slice carrots. Cut partially frozen steak into paper-thin slices. Arrange beef and vegetables attractively on platters; cover and keep refrigerated until serving.

Bring the chicken stock to a boil in a fondue pot on the stove. Transfer the pot to a table-top burner and keep at HIGH heat. Using chopsticks or fondue forks, wave a slice of meat or vegetable back and forth in the stock for a few seconds. (The meat should still be pink when it is eaten.)

Sesame Seed Sauce (page 123) is the perfect dip.

# ❖ BROTH ORIENTALE ❖

When you finish eating all the meat and solids of your Fondue
Orientale, Fondue Chinoise, or Fondue Japonaise, the remaining broth
may be used as a delicious post-entree soup.

> *½ cup (120 ml) dry sherry* OR *dry white wine*
> *salt and pepper to taste*
> *fondue broth*

Combine sherry or wine and salt and pepper with the broth. Stir
well and heat. Serve in mugs.

# ❖ ASIAN HOT POT ❖

Makes 6 servings

*2 pieces ginger root*

*2 Tbsp rice wine*

*1 tsp sesame oil*

*1 lb (450 g) chicken breasts*

*½ lb (225 g) shrimp*

*12 fresh shiitake mushrooms*

*24 small florets broccoli, cauliflower, OR both*

*4 cups (960 ml) chicken stock, preferably homemade*

## PREPARING THE BROTH

Smash the ginger root and add to stock in a large saucepan along with the rice wine and sesame oil. Cook about 5 minutes. Discard the ginger root and transfer broth to a fondue pot to cook the dunkable chicken slices, shrimp, vegetables, and mushrooms.

Prepare the soup (page 77).

## PREPARING THE DUNKABLES

Slice chicken breasts into very thin strips. Clean and butterfly the shrimp. Remove stems from mushrooms.

## SOUP

*4 oz (110 g) rice noodles*

*4 oz (110 g) fresh spinach*

*3 green onions*

*4 oz (110 g) bean sprouts*

*2 Tbsp soy sauce*

*salt and pepper*

## PREPARING THE POST-ENTREE SOUP

Soak rice noodles in hot water for 10 minutes and drain well. Chop the spinach and slice the onions. When everyone has finished eating, add the noodles, spinach, onions, bean sprouts, and soy sauce to the stock mixture. Adjust seasoning to taste and reheat. Serve in bowls or mugs.

## SERVING SUGGESTIONS

Sauce Orientale (page 121), Shanghai Sweet and Sour Sauce (page 124), Soy-Wasabi Sauce (page 125), Spicy Red Apple Sauce (page 126) and Teriyaki Sauce (page 128).

# Fish, Fowl, and Pizza

## Some unusual fondue mixtures

*The recipes in this chapter are the best proof that the fondue is a most flexible dish and that anyone with culinary imagination can dream up variations that will tickle the taste buds of even the most blasé diner.*

*With a little imagination and some leftovers, a book the length of this one could be compiled with fondue recipes that would not only prove tongue-titillating but would also keep the budget in check in any kitchen in the land.*

*Cooked-meat leftovers, or meatballs, will give excellent results. In the case of meatballs, remember to keep them mildly seasoned and firm, and the sauces spicy. Disguise leftover meats such as chicken, turkey, or pork in delicately seasoned Fondue Batter (page 96) before cooking them in hot oil.*

### Serving Suggestion

*The sauces that go best with fish are tangy—such as Cocktail Sauce (page 111), Sauce Aurore (page 120), Tartar-Relish Sauce (page 127), Tomato Paprika Sauce (page 128), or your own favorite bottled seafood sauces.*

# ❖ FISH AND SEAFOOD FONDUE ❖
### Makes 3 to 4 servings

*8 oz (225 g) fish fillets*

*8 oz (225 g) shelled lobster*

*8 oz (225 g) peeled and cleaned shrimp*

*salad oil*

*1 tsp salt*

Drain uncooked fish and seafood thoroughly; pat dry with paper toweling. Cut into bite-size pieces (about 1 inch or 2.5 cm). Heat oil to 375°F (190°C). Add salt to oil. Fry fish until lightly browned on a fondue fork.

# ❖ HERBED SHRIMP FONDUE ❖
### Makes 4 to 6 servings

*two 4-oz (110 g) cans tiny shrimp,* OR *shrimp bits and pieces, undrained*

*10-oz (280-g) can frozen cream of shrimp soup*

*2 Tbsp butter*

*3-oz (85-g) package cream cheese at room temperature*

*¼ cup (60 ml) parsley, finely chopped*

*¼ cup (60 ml) sherry*

*1 Tbsp cornstarch*

*⅛ tsp crushed tarragon leaves*

*⅛ tsp celery salt*

*⅛ tsp freshly ground pepper*

Drain the liquid from the cans of shrimp into a fondue pot. Add frozen cream of shrimp soup and place over LOW heat. Stir occasionally until soup is melted. Chop the drained shrimp to the size of cooked rice grains and stir them into the mixture. Add butter and cream cheese and stir until both have melted and the mixture is smoothly blended. Add parsley, mixing in thoroughly.

Combine sherry and cornstarch, stirring until free of lumps, and add to the shrimp. Mix well. Add tarragon, celery salt, and pepper and stir until mixture has thickened slightly.

## SERVING SUGGESTION

Saltines make a good dunkable, along with bread cubes.

# ❖ SHRIMP AND AVOCADO FONDUE ❖

Makes 4 servings

*4 oz (110 g) butter* OR *margarine*

*½ cup (120 ml) onion, minced*

*1 clove garlic, minced*

*½ cup (120 ml) all-purpose flour*

*¾ cup (180 ml) milk*

*¾ cup (180 ml) cream*

*1 tsp salt*

*¼ tsp black pepper*

*⅓ cup (80 ml) lemon juice*

*large avocado, mashed*

*½ cup (120 ml) Parmesan cheese, grated*

*2 Tbsp dry sherry*

*1 lb (450 g) shrimp, peeled and cooked*

Melt the butter in a fondue pot; then add onion and garlic, cooking until the onion is soft. Stir in flour and continue cooking for 2 minutes over LOW heat. Remove the pot from heat; add milk and cream, stirring constantly. Add salt, pepper, lemon juice, and avocado, stirring constantly over LOW heat for 5 minutes. Add cheese and stir well until cheese has melted. Add sherry.

Use peeled, cooked shrimp for dunking.

# ❖ SCALLOPS AND FISH FONDUE ❖

### Makes 4 to 6 servings

*½ lb (225 g) salmon, cut in 1-inch (2.5-cm) cubes*

*½ lb (225 g) monkfish, cut in 1-inch (2.5-cm) cubes*

*¼ lb (110 g) scallops*

*½ lb (225 g) medium-large shrimps, shelled and deveined*

*salt*

*lemon wedges and coriander for garnish*

*½ cup (120 ml) onion, finely chopped*

*2 cloves garlic, finely minced*

*2 tsp ginger, grated*

*2 Tbsp butter*

*2 cups (480 ml) dry white wine*

*2 cups (480 ml) water*

*1 tsp salt*

*½ cup (125 ml) coriander stems, chopped*

Salt lightly and chill seafood until ready to serve. Garnish with lemon and coriander. Sauté onion, garlic and ginger in butter until soft. Do not brown. Add wine, water, salt, and coriander stems. Bring to a boil and transfer to fondue pot. Poach dunkables lightly, being careful not to overcook.

### SERVING SUGGESTION

These dipping sauces are spicy and add to the contrasting colors, textures, and flavors of the seafood: Chili-Peanut Sauce (page 111), Soy-Wasabi Sauce (page 125), and Provençal Rouille (page 119).

# ❖ CLAM FONDUE ❖

Makes 4 to 6 servings

*7-oz (195–200-g) can minced clams, drained*

*4 Tbsp butter*

*¼ cup (60 ml) scallions, finely chopped*

*¼ cup (60 ml) green pepper, finely chopped*

*⅓ cup (80 ml) ketchup*

*2 cups (480 ml) grated mild Cheddar cheese*

*1 Tbsp Worcestershire sauce*

Chop the clams until they are the size of cooked rice grains. Melt butter in a fondue pot over moderate heat. When the butter is bubbling, add scallions and green pepper, and cook until the pepper becomes transparent. Add clams and ketchup to the butter mixture and cook until mixture begins to bubble again.

Turn heat to LOW; add cheese, about a ½ cup (120 ml) at a time, stirring well after each addition until the mixture is creamy. Add Worcestershire sauce and mix thoroughly.

## SERVING SUGGESTION

Saltines may be substituted for (or accompany) bite-size French or Italian bread as dunkables.

## ❖ QUICK CLAM FONDUE ❖

Makes 4 to 6 servings

*7-oz (195–200-g) can minced clams, drained*
*10-fl-oz (300-ml) can tomato soup*
*10-fl-oz (300-ml) can green pea soup*
*8-oz (225-g) package cream cheese*
*3 Tbsp sherry*

Chop the clams until they are the size of cooked rice grains. Empty the cans of tomato and pea soup into a fondue pot over MODERATE heat.

Add the cream cheese and cook until it has melted and the mixture is creamy. Turn the heat to low, add the chopped clams, and continue to cook for 5 minutes. Stir in the sherry.

## ❖ SHRIMP FONDUE ❖

Makes 4 servings

*10-fl-oz (300-ml) can frozen shrimp soup OR cream of shrimp soup*
*1 cup (240 g) Swiss cheese, shredded*
*2 Tbsp dry white wine*

Heat the soup in top of a double boiler over boiling water. Add cheese, stirring occasionally until melted. Transfer to a fondue pot; stir in wine.

# ❖ SHRIMP IN CURRY FONDUE ❖

Makes 6 servings

*3 lb (1.5 kg) large, raw* OR *thawed shrimp, cleaned*
*olive oil*
*¾ cup (180 ml) lemon juice*
*salt and pepper*
*curry sauce* OR *mild curry sauce*

Rinse the shrimp in cold water; pat dry with paper toweling. Fill the fondue pot halfway with oil; bring to bubbling point. Cook shrimp to individual taste on a fondue fork.

Dip cooked shrimp in lemon juice, sprinkle with salt and pepper to taste; then dip in Curry Sauce (page 112) or Mild Curry Sauce (page 117).

### SERVING SUGGESTION

An interesting accompaniment to this curry dish is coleslaw mixed with caraway seeds.

# ❖ CRABMEAT FONDUE I ❖

**Makes 4 servings**

*7½-oz (210-g) can crabmeat, drained*

*8-oz (225-g) package cream cheese, at room temperature*

*dash garlic powder*

*¼ cup (60 ml) mayonnaise*

*¼ tsp dry mustard*

*¼ tsp granulated sugar*

*¼ tsp seasoned salt*

*2 Tbsp white wine*

Chop the crabmeat to pieces the size of cooked rice grains. Add the cream cheese, garlic powder, and mayonnaise. Mix and beat with a fork until smoothly blended.

Put the mixture in a fondue pot over LOW heat; cook and stir until melted and creamy. Add dry mustard, sugar, and salt and stir while cooking for a few minutes longer. Add white wine.

# ❖ CRABMEAT FONDUE II ❖

Makes 4 servings

*7½-oz (210-g) can crabmeat, drained and cartilage removed*

*3-oz (85-g) package cream cheese, at room temperature*

*10-fl-oz (300-ml) can condensed cream of mushroom soup*

*3 Tbsp heavy cream*

*3 Tbsp sherry*

Chop crabmeat finely into pieces the size of cooked rice grains. Place cream cheese and mushroom soup in a fondue pot over MODERATE heat; stir until well mixed, creamy, and steaming hot.

Add cream gradually and mix well; turn heat to LOW.

Add crabmeat and mix well; continue cooking at LOW heat for 5 minutes, stirring frequently. Stir in the sherry and serve.

# ❖ CRABMEAT FONDUE III ❖

Makes 4 to 6 servings

*8-oz (225-g) package Velveeta processed cheese*

*5-oz (140-g) package Old English cheese*

*3 Tbsp heavy cream*

*4-oz (110-g) can mushroom stems and pieces, drained*

*7½-oz (210-g) can crabmeat, drained and cartilage removed*

*4½-oz (125-g) can ripe sliced olives, drained*

*3 Tbsp sherry*

*1 drop Tabasco sauce*

Place cheeses in a fondue pot over LOW heat, stirring frequently until the cheese is melted. Add the cream and mix well.

Place the mushrooms, crabmeat, and olives in a bowl and chop until the size of small peas; add to the cheese mixture. Mix well until heated thoroughly.

Add the sherry and Tabasco; stir frequently for another 5 minutes.

## SERVING SUGGESTION

This fondue can be served with cooked cauliflower and broccoli florets. See serving suggestions for Bagna Cauda (page 104). Saltines can be used as dunkables in addition to bite-size pieces of French bread.

# ❖ CRABMEAT FONDUE IV ❖

Makes 4 to 6 servings

*1 frozen haddock fillet, skinless (6 x 3 x ½ inch)*

*4 oz (110 g) butter*

*1 tsp onion, grated*

*8-oz (225-g) package cream cheese, at room temperature*

*4 oz (110 g) American process cheese, grated*

*2 Tbsp cream*

*7½-oz (210-g) can crabmeat, drained*

Place haddock in a skillet with about ½ inch (1.25 cm) slightly salted boiling water. Bring to a rolling boil; then turn fillet over and boil for an additional 3 minutes, or until fork can be easily twisted in the thickest part. Drain well and set aside to cool.

Melt the butter in a fondue pot over LOW heat; add the onion and cook on LOW heat for 5 minutes. Add the cream cheese; stir and cook until completely melted. Add half the American cheese, stirring until completely melted; then add the other half and repeat the process until the mixture is smooth and creamy. Add the cream and mix well.

Flake the cooled haddock until well broken up, discarding any tough portions and any remaining skin. Remove any cartilage from the crabmeat and add the crabmeat to the haddock in a bowl. Chop until both reach the consistency of raw rice grains. Add the fish mixture to the cheese mixture, mix well, and continue to cook at LOW heat for 3 minutes, or until heated through. Stir frequently.

## SERVING SUGGESTION

Serve with chunks of crisp French bread, triangles of toast, wedges of toasted English muffins, or saltines.

# ❖ SALMON FONDUE ❖

Makes 4 servings

2 Tbsp butter OR margarine

1 clove garlic, minced

2 Tbsp minced onion

8 oz (225 g) fresh mushrooms, thinly sliced

½ tsp salt

¼ tsp white pepper

2 cups (480 ml) canned salmon, drained and flaked

¼ cup (60 ml) dry sherry

4 large egg yolks

1½ cups (360 ml) cream

½ cup (120 ml) grated Parmesan cheese

¼ cup (60 ml) minced parsley

Melt the butter in a fondue pot. Add garlic and onions and sauté for 1 minute. Add mushrooms and cook 3 to 5 minutes, stirring frequently. Add salt, pepper, salmon and sherry.

Beat the egg yolks with the cream, Parmesan, and parsley; add over LOW heat, stirring constantly for about 5 minutes.

# ❖ SALMON CHEESE FONDUE ❖

Makes 4 servings

4 oz (110 g) butter OR margarine

1½ cups (360 ml) onion, minced

1 clove garlic, minced

2 Tbsp chopped parsley

2 cups (480 ml) Swiss cheese, grated

2 cups (480 ml) Cheddar cheese, grated

¾ cup (180 ml) tomato sauce

¼ cup (60 ml) Worcestershire sauce

¼ cup (60 ml) brandy

1 tsp salt

¼ tsp white pepper

1½ cups (12 fl oz or 360 ml) canned salmon, drained

Melt the butter in a fondue pot. Add the onions and garlic and sauté until the onions are very soft. Add the parsley and both cheeses, stirring constantly until the cheeses melt and the mixture starts to bubble.

Add the tomato sauce, Worcestershire sauce, brandy, salt, and pepper and mix thoroughly. Add the salmon and mix well. Cook over LOW heat for about 4 minutes.

# ❖ TUNA FONDUE ❖

### Makes 4 servings

*1 clove garlic, halved*

*2 cups (480 ml) dry white wine*

*8 oz (225 g) Swiss cheese, diced*

*8 oz (225 g) Gruyère cheese, diced*

*1½ Tbsp (22.5 ml) cornstarch*

*2 Tbsp kirsch OR brandy*

*nutmeg*

*6½-oz (185-g) can tuna, drained and flaked*

*bread dunkables*

Rub a fondue pot with garlic. Add wine and warm over MEDIUM heat—DO NOT BOIL. Add cheese by handfuls, stirring constantly as cheese melts. Blend cornstarch and liquor, with nutmeg to taste, into cheese mixture when it begins to bubble. Add tuna, stirring constantly for 1 minute.

# ❖ TUNA CROQUETTES ❖

Makes 4 to 5 servings (10 to 12 as an appetizer)

*6-oz (170-g) can solid white meat tuna*

*2 large eggs*

*¼ cup (60 ml) shredded carrot*

*¼ cup (60 ml) chopped onion*

*¼ tsp salt*

*¼ tsp pepper*

*flour*

*cornflake crumbs* OR *packaged dried bread crumbs*

*4 cups (960 ml) salad oil*

Drain and flake tuna. Beat 1 egg and add carrot, onion, salt, and pepper and tuna. Mix together well and shape into balls, each containing about 1 teaspoon.

Use a fork to beat the second egg in a pie plate until foamy. Roll each tuna ball in flour until completely coated. Dip the tuna balls into the beaten egg; then roll in the cornflake or bread crumbs. When all the tuna balls are coated, refrigerate for at least 4 hours to firm and set.

Pour salad oil into a fondue pot and bring to 425°F (220°C), using a deep-fry thermometer. Cook the croquettes held on fondue forks.

## SERVING SUGGESTIONS

Try these sauces suitable with the tuna croquettes: Sauce Tartare De Luxe (page 122), Tartar-Relish Sauce (page 127), and Sauce Diable (page 120), and prepared tartar sauce.

# ❖ POULTRY AND SEAFOOD FONDUE ❖

Makes 4 servings

*1 package onion soup mix*

*4 cups (960 ml) boiling water*

*1 cup (240 ml) red wine*

*3 Tbsp chili sauce*

*juice of one lemon*

*⅓ cup (80 ml) finely chopped fresh parsley*

*½ lb (225 g) filleted steak*

*½ lb (225 g) uncooked chicken OR turkey breast, sliced very thin*

*½ lb (225 g) uncooked large shrimp, shelled and deveined*

*½ lb (225 g) uncooked scallops*

*1 large egg (optional)*

Stir soup mix into boiling water. Add wine, chili sauce, and lemon juice. Bring to a boil and simmer uncovered for about 1 hour. Add parsley and pour into a fondue pot.

Break the egg into the fondue pot when the poultry and seafood are eaten, stir well and serve as soup in small bowls.

## ❖ LOBSTER FONDUE ❖

Makes 3 to 4 servings.

*10-fl-oz (300-ml) can frozen condensed cream of shrimp soup*
*⅝ cup ( 5 fl oz or 150 ml) milk*
*½ cup (120 ml) shredded sharp cheese*
*½ cup (120 ml) cooked* OR *canned lobster, cut into bite-size pieces*
*dash paprika*
*dash cayenne*
*2 Tbsp sherry*

Combine soup and milk in a chafing dish or saucepan; heat slowly until the soup is thawed. Add cheese, lobster, paprika, and cayenne. Heat, stirring often until the cheese melts. Add sherry.

## ❖ CHICKEN FONDUE ❖

*corn oil*
*¾ cup (180 ml) per person cooked chicken,*
*cut into ¾-inch (2-cm) cubes per person*
*Fondue Batter (page 96)*

Fill a fondue pot with oil about halfway and heat until bubbling.
Spear chicken on a fondue fork, dip into batter, then plunge into oil. Leave in the oil until the batter puffs, crisps, and browns. Transfer to an individual plate. Dip into a sauce of choice.

# ❖ FONDUE BATTER ❖

Makes about 2 cups (480 ml)

*¾ cup (180 ml) all-purpose flour*

*¼ cup (60 ml) cornstarch*

*1 tsp baking powder*

*2 tsp salt*

*½ tsp nutmeg*

*2 large eggs*

*½ cup (120 ml) beer*

Mix the dry ingredients together. Add the eggs and beer; beat until the batter is smooth.

## SERVING SUGGESTIONS

This makes a fine dipping batter for chicken cubes, and it makes a tasty coating for such dunkables as cubes of leftover turkey, sliced frankfurters, and cocktail franks.

This beer batter can be used with beef or other meats, shrimp, and cubes of Gouda or Edam cheese. It also makes a striking combination with pineapple, bananas, or pieces of other fruit. Best of all, why not have a selection of several or many of these dunkables and let your guests select as their taste dictates at the moment.

# ❖ FONDUE FOIE DE POULET ❖

Makes 4 to 6 servings

*1½ lb (675 g) chicken livers*
*½ lb (225 g) fresh mushroom caps*
*4 medium potatoes*
*water*
*1 Tbsp lemon juice*
*1½ lb (675 g) fresh asparagus*
*½ bunch parsley*
*1 cup (240 ml) vegetable oil*
*8 oz (225 g) butter* OR *margarine*

Clean chicken livers and cut into ¾-inch (2-cm) chunks. Clean mushrooms and cut into ¼-inch (1-cm) slices. Peel potatoes and cut into ¼-inch (1-cm) slices; soak in water with lemon juice to keep from turning brown. Clean asparagus and partially cook, drain, and cut into 1-inch (2.5-cm) pieces. Chop parsley finely. Heat oil and butter until bubbling, but not foaming.

## SERVING SUGGESTION

Diners spear a piece of chicken liver, mushroom, potato, or asparagus and cook it for about 1 minute, or to taste. Then dip the chicken livers and potatoes in the chopped parsley, and dip the mushrooms and asparagus in a Simple Hollandaise Sauce (page 125).

# ❖ PIZZA FONDUE ❖

Makes 4 to 6 servings

*2 Tbsp butter*

*¾ cup (180 ml) onion, finely chopped*

*½ lb (225 g) lean ground chuck*

*14-fl-oz (420-ml) can tomato sauce*

*6-fl-oz (180-ml) can chili-pepper-flavored tomato juice*

*8 oz (225 g) grated Mozzarella cheese*

*4 oz (110 g) grated American process cheese*

*3 Tbsp cornstarch*

*1 tsp fennel seed*

*½ tsp sweet basil*

*½ tsp oregano*

Melt butter in a fondue pot over MODERATE heat until sizzling hot. Add chopped onion and sauté until it becomes limp and transparent.

Add the ground chuck; sauté and stir until it completely breaks apart and begins to brown slightly. Add the tomato sauce and tomato juice; mix thoroughly. Continue to cook over MODERATE heat, stirring occasionally until the sauce begins to bubble; turn heat to LOW.

Place the two grated cheeses in a bowl and sprinkle with the cornstarch; toss thoroughly until uniformly mixed. Add the cheese mixture to the beef-tomato sauce, ½ cup (120 ml) at a time, stirring well each time until the cheese has melted completely. Add the fennel seeds, basil, and oregano, mixing well. Continue cooking over LOW heat, stirring frequently, for 5 minutes or so until the flavors are completely melded.

Dunk bread cubes or wedges of lightly toasted English muffins.

# ❖ PEPPERONI PIZZA ❖

Makes 4 to 6 servings

½ lb (225 g) fresh Italian pork sausage

1 cup (240 ml) finely chopped purple onion

14-fl-oz (420-ml) can tomato sauce with cheese

6-fl-oz (180-ml) can tomato paste

¼ cup (60 ml) water

1 tsp fennel seed

½ tsp each of oregano, sweet basil, salt

$\frac{1}{16}$ tsp freshly ground pepper

8 oz (225 g) Mozzarella cheese

4 oz (110 g) grated sharp Cheddar cheese

2 oz (55 g) grated Parmesan cheese

3 Tbsp cornstarch

½ cup (120 ml) finely diced pepperoni sausage

Remove the casings from the pork sausage and cut the sausage into ½-inch (1-cm) slices. Cook in a fondue pot over MODERATE heat and sauté until sausage loses its reddish color and completely breaks apart. Pour off and discard all but 1 Tbsp of the grease. Add the chopped onion; sauté over MODERATE heat until onion becomes limp and transparent.

Add the tomato sauce, tomato paste, and water; mix well and continue to cook over MODERATE heat until the mixture begins to bubble. Add the fennel seed, oregano, basil, salt, and pepper. Mix thoroughly. Turn the heat to LOW and cook for 3 minutes, stirring occasionally.

Blend the three cheeses thoroughly with the cornstarch. Add ½ cup (120 ml) at a time, stirring after each addition until the cheese completely melts. Add the pepperoni and cook 5 minutes, stirring frequently.

# ❖ FRANKFURTER PIZZA FONDUE ❖

Makes 4 servings

*2 Tbsp butter*

*2 Tbsp flour*

*½ tsp salt*

*½ tsp garlic salt*

*2 cups (480 ml) milk*

*8 oz (225 g) mozzarella* OR *Swiss cheese, diced*

*1¼ tsp (6 ml) oregano*

*1 tsp basil*

*1 lb (450 g) cooked frankfurters* OR *Italian sausage*

Melt butter in a saucepan. Stir in flour, salt, and garlic salt until smooth. Add milk slowly, stirring constantly until smooth and thickened. Reduce heat and gradually add cheese and herbs, stirring until cheese is just melted. Pour into a fondue pot. Place over LOW heat.

Heat frankfurters or sausage in boiling water; cut diagonally into 1-inch (2.5-cm) slices. Keep frankfurters or sausage warm in a chafing dish or casserole over a flame or hot plate. Spear meat on a fondue fork and dip into the fondue.

## SERVING SUGGESTION

Serve with slices of buttered hot French bread, or such dunkables as raw cauliflower, cherry tomatoes, tomato wedges, or potato chips.

# ❖ BACON PIZZA ❖

Makes 4 servings

*six 10-inch (25-cm) thin slices lean bacon*
*½ cup (120 ml) finely chopped onion*
*1 clove garlic, finely chopped*
*14-fl-oz (420-ml) can tomato sauce*
*¼ tsp oregano*
*¼ tsp sweet basil*
*¼ tsp fennel seed*
*8 oz (225 g) mild American cheese, grated*
*1 Tbsp cornstarch*

Dice the bacon into ¼-inch (0.5-cm) squares and place in the bottom of a fondue pot over MODERATE heat. Sauté until crisp and golden. Drain off and discard all but 1 Tbsp of the fat.

Add onion and continue to sauté until the onion becomes limp and slightly transparent. Add garlic, tomato sauce, oregano, basil, and fennel seed. Mix well over moderate heat and cook until the sauce begins to bubble. Turn heat to LOW.

Toss the cheese with the cornstarch until uniformly mixed. Add this mixture to the sauce about ½ cup (120 ml) at a time, stirring after each addition until cheese has melted. Continue to cook on LOW heat for 5 minutes, stirring frequently.

## SERVING SUGGESTION

Wedges of toasted English muffin make ideal dunkables.

# ❖ QUICK PIZZA FONDUE ❖

Makes 6 to 8 servings

*19-fl-oz (570-ml) can seasoned stewed tomatoes, with juice*

*½ tsp Tabasco sauce, or to taste*

*¾ tsp salt*

*8 oz (225 g) process cheese, shredded*

*⅓ cup (80 ml) diced green pepper*

*bread dunkables*

Combine tomatoes, Tabasco sauce, and salt in a heavy saucepan. Place over LOW heat and bring to a boil; reduce heat immediately and simmer for 5 minutes to blend flavors.

Stir in cheese and cook, stirring constantly, for 1 minute or until the cheese has melted.

Pour into a fondue pot; garnish with green peppers.

# Vegetable Fondues

## Crudités in delectable sauces

*R*aw *seasonable vegetable chunks served in fondue fashion is a dish credited with having been developed in the Piedmont region of Italy. The tradition calls for placing the raw vegetable dunkables in ice water for a short time to make them crisp. While this leeches out some vitamins, the Piedmontese claim it has the effect of cooling the sauce and preventing possible damage to the tender tissues of the mouth.*

*Crudités—as we employ the term for vegetables served in this manner at cocktail parties or as an appetizer—is a French word indicating "rawness." The French dish is usually served with a cold sauce (such as mayonnaise). But it was the Italians who delectably combined that concept with the Swiss hot-sauce idea and called it Bagna Cauda (literally "hot bath" or "warm bath"). And they added to the pleasures of the veggie fondue by using some vegetable dunkables that have been cooked.*

*Spear the veggies onto a fondue fork and place them in the fondue pot for a moment or two. Hold a bread cube in the other hand to catch the savory drips of vegetable stock or the olive oil from the hot dunkables.*

# ❖ BAGNA CAUDA ❖

Makes 4 servings

*½ cup (120 ml) olive oil*

*4 oz (110 g) butter*

*3 medium cloves garlic, finely chopped*

*1.65-oz (45-g) can flat anchovy fillets, finely chopped, with oil*

*½ tsp salt*

*⅛ tsp red pepper flakes*

Combine olive oil and butter in a fondue pot. Heat oil until the butter begins to melt. Add garlic, chopped anchovy fillets with their oil, salt, and red pepper flakes. Heat gently over LOW heat for about 10 minutes, stirring occasionally, until the garlic is soft and anchovies are dissolved.

## SERVING SUGGESTIONS

Use cubes of bread to catch the savory drips of oil from vegetables.

Raw vegetables for dipping can include red, green, and yellow pepper pieces; celery strips; carrot slices or thin baby carrots; small mushroom caps; zucchini or yellow summer squash slices; jicama slices; green onions; and cucumber slices.

Some cooked vegetables great for dipping include snow peas and broccoli or cauliflower florets. Blanch them for 1 minute in boiling water or microwave them briefly.

Serve with small new potatoes.

# ❖ SWEET CORN FONDUE ❖

Makes 4 servings

*2 Tbsp water*
*1 lb (450 g) frozen corn kernels*
*2 tsp corn flour*
*3 Tbsp light cream*
*salt and pepper*
*Tabasco sauce*
*2 Tbsp butter*

Put the water in a saucepan, add the corn kernels, and allow them to simmer a few minutes until tender. Drain the corn and then place it in a food blender and process until soft, but not too smooth.

Mix the corn flour and cream in a second saucepan, blending until smooth. Add the corn kernel mixture, cooking over LOW heat until smooth. Pour the mixture into a fondue pot, add salt and pepper to taste, and add a few drops of Tabasco. Beat in the butter and set the fondue pot into a holder over a LOW fire to keep warm.

Serve with a variety of raw vegetables.

# ❖ GOLDEN VEGETABLE FONDUE ❖

Makes 4 servings

*1¼ cups (300 ml) vegetable stock\**
*8 oz (225 g) carrots*
*small turnip*
*½ medium size rutabaga*
*2 stalks celery*
*small onion*
*4 Tbsp butter*
*salt and pepper*
*freshly grated nutmeg*

Chop the vegetables finely and add to the stock in a saucepan. Bring to a boil and simmer until the vegetables are just tender; then drain them and let them cool slightly. Transfer the stock into a fondue pot.

Puree the vegetables in a blender or food processor, then pass the puree through a sieve into the stock.

Place the pot over LOW heat and keep the mixture hot while cutting the butter into small chunks. Add a few chunks at a time, beating all the while until they have melted. Add salt and pepper and a pinch of nutmeg to taste.

Serve with small cooked potatoes, which may be either hot or cold.

*Use canned vegetable broth or homemade stock.

# Sauces Sweet and Spicy

Dips for your meat dishes

*A meat fondue is nothing at all without the accompanying sauces. There are, of course, the traditional Béarnaise and Hollandaise, and there are such simple adornments as mustard, ketchup, and horseradish. But besides these, there are countless possibilities.*

*With fondues, there is no question—the more sauces, the merrier. So be imaginative; offer several simple sauces, or go all out with a half-dozen or more zingy ones. You can invent dozens of combinations to make your repertoire of sauces delightfully unique.*

*At the end of this chapter, we suggest a few of the many kinds of prepared relishes and sauces that will help extend your culinary inventiveness. So follow some recipes here, or create combinations of your own. Be saucy!*

# ❖ BÉARNAISE SAUCE ❖

Makes about 1 cup (240 ml)

*1 Tbsp finely chopped shallots*
*1 tsp chopped fresh parsley*
*¼ tsp dried tarragon*
*¼ tsp dried thyme*
*pinch black pepper*
*pinch salt*
*¼ cup (60 ml) dry white wine*
*¼ cup (60 ml) tarragon vinegar*
*3 egg yolks*
*slightly melted butter, as required*

Add shallots, parsley, and seasonings to wine and vinegar in a saucepan. Boil rapidly until reduced by half. Strain liquid and cool.

Beat in egg yolks, one at a time, alternating with as much of the slightly melted butter as necessary to keep the sauce at the consistency of mayonnaise.

Serve cold.

# ❖ BORDELAISE SAUCE ❖

Makes about 2 cups (480 ml)

*4 shallots, finely chopped*

*6 peppercorns, crushed*

*2 parsley sprigs*

*½ tsp dried thyme*

*bay leaf*

*1 tsp finely chopped garlic*

*1 cup (240 ml) dry red wine*

*1¼ cups (300 ml) brown sauce* OR *canned beef gravy*

*salt and freshly ground pepper, to taste*

*juice of 1 lemon*

*2 Tbsp butter*

Combine shallots, peppercorns, parsley, thyme, bay leaf, garlic, and wine in a saucepan. Cook over MODERATELY HIGH heat until reduced by half.

Stir in the brown sauce and simmer for about 10 minutes. Add salt and pepper. Strain through a sieve and bring to a boil again. Stir in lemon juice and remove from heat. Swirl in butter.

Serve hot.

## ❖ BROWN MUSHROOM SAUCE ❖

Makes about 1⅓ cups (325 ml)

*2 Tbsp butter*
*2 Tbsp flour*
*⅔ cup (160 ml) consommé*
*1 tsp Worcestershire sauce*
*½ cup (120 ml) finely chopped mushrooms*
*½ cup (120 ml) sour cream*

Melt butter in a saucepan; blend in flour. Remove from heat and gradually stir in consommé. Return to heat and stir until thickened. Blend in the remaining ingredients. Serve hot.

## ❖ CALIFORNIA DIP ❖

Makes about 2 cups (480 ml)

*1 package onion soup mix*
*2 cups (1 pint or 500 ml) sour cream*

Mix the onion soup mix and the sour cream well.

# ❖ CHILI-PEANUT SAUCE ❖

Makes about 1⅓ cups (300 ml)

*½ tsp dried red chili flakes*

*1 clove garlic, minced*

*2 Tbsp vegetable oil*

*2 Tbsp lemon grass, finely sliced*

*1 tsp grated ginger*

*¼ cup (60 ml) peanut butter, smooth OR crunchy*

*½ cup (120 ml) coconut milk*

*2 to 4 Tbsp (30–60 ml) medium sherry, to taste*

Sauté chili flakes and garlic in oil; do not brown the garlic. Add lemon grass, ginger, peanut butter, and coconut milk. Simmer about 10 minutes until thickened. Dilute the fondue mixture to the consistency of soft butter with the sherry—just before serving. Serve warm.

# ❖ COCKTAIL SAUCE ❖

Makes about ¾ cup (180 ml)

*1 Tbsp fresh OR bottled horseradish*

*1 Tbsp lemon juice*

*1 tsp Worcestershire sauce*

*¾ cup (180 ml) ketchup*

*Tabasco sauce*

*salt and freshly ground pepper to taste*

Combine all ingredients in a bowl and mix well.

## ❖ CURRY SAUCE ❖

*8 oz (225 g) butter*

*1 cup (240 ml) flour*

*1½ tsp curry powder*

*1 Tbsp lemon juice*

*10-fl-oz (300-ml) can consommé*

*2 Tbsp water*

Melt butter, stir in flour, and remove from heat. Combine curry powder and lemon juice. Add to butter-flour mixture, stirring well. Return
to LOW heat and simmer for about 2 minutes, stirring constantly.

Mix consommé with water; add gradually and continue cooking
over LOW heat, stirring constantly for about 15 minutes.

## ❖ GARLIC SAUCE ❖

Makes about 1 cup (240 ml)

*4 large cloves garlic*

*2 large egg yolks*

*1 cup (240 ml) olive oil*

*1 tsp lemon juice*

*¼ tsp salt*

*¼ tsp freshly ground black pepper*

Mash the garlic with egg yolks in a bowl. Beat in the olive oil drop by
drop until the sauce reaches the consistency of mayonnaise. Stir in
lemon juice, salt, and pepper.

# ❖ GREEN SAUCE ❖

Makes about 1 cup (240 ml)

*1 slice white bread, crust removed*

*¼ cup (60 ml) white vinegar*

*3 anchovy fillets, finely chopped* OR *½ tsp anchovy paste*

*1 cup (240 ml) finely chopped fresh parsley*

*1½ tsp chopped capers*

*2 cloves garlic, crushed*

*1½ tsp grated onion*

*4 tsp olive oil*

*½ tsp sugar*

*2 Tbsp vinegar*

Soak the bread in a bowl with ¼ cup (60 ml) vinegar. Mix in anchovy fillets or paste, parsley, capers, garlic, onion, olive oil, and sugar. Mash and beat into a smooth paste. Stir in 2 Tbsp vinegar—and more oil if desired to achieve preferred consistency.

# OLIVE SAUCE

Follow the recipe for Green Sauce and add 2 Tbsp coarsely chopped pitted green olives with the anchovies, parsley, capers, garlic, onion, olive oil, and sugar.

# PICKLE SAUCE

Follow the recipe for Green Sauce and add 2 Tbsp chopped pickles with the anchovies, parsley, capers, garlic, onion, olive oil, and sugar.

# PEPPER SAUCE

Follow the Green Sauce recipe and add 2 Tbsp chopped green pepper with the anchovies, parsley, capers, garlic, onion, olive oil, and sugar.

# ❖ HORSERADISH DIP ❖

Makes about 1 cup (240 ml)

*1 cup (240 ml) California Dip*

*1 Tbsp horseradish*

*2 Tbsp milk*

*parsley*

Combine California Dip (page 110) with horseradish and milk. Sprinkle snippings of parsley over the top.

## ❖ HORSERADISH AND MAYONNAISE ❖

Makes 1 cup (240 ml)

*½ cup (120 ml) mayonnaise*

*3 Tbsp prepared horseradish*

*½ cup (120 ml) chili sauce*

Combine the mayonnaise, horseradish, and chili sauce.


## ❖ HORSERADISH AND SOUR CREAM SAUCE ❖

Makes about ¾ cup (180 ml)

*1 Tbsp freshly grated horseradish*

*¾ cup sour cream*

*1 Tbsp finely chopped onion*

Combine all ingredients in a bowl and mix well.


### NOTE

If fresh horseradish is not available, use bottled horseradish. Use cheesecloth to squeeze and remove as much vinegar as you can.

## ❖ HOT PAPRIKA SAUCE ❖

Makes about 1 cup (240 ml)

*2 Tbsp butter, softened*

*½ tsp salt*

*3 Tbsp flour*

*white pepper*

*1 cup (240 ml) hot milk*

*1 Tbsp hot Hungarian paprika, OR to taste*

Combine all ingredients, except paprika, in a blender and turn to LOW speed. When blades have reached full momentum, switch the motor to HIGH and blend further for 30 seconds.

Pour the mixture into the top of a double boiler and cook over simmering water for 15 minutes, stirring occasionally. Stir in paprika to taste. The sauce should look quite pink.

## ❖ ITALIAN SAUCE ❖

Makes about 1 cup (240 ml)

*1 cup or 8-fl-oz (240-ml) can tomato sauce with cheese*

*1 Tbsp freshly ground black pepper*

*½ tsp oregano*

*½ tsp garlic salt*

Combine all ingredients and simmer for 15 minutes, stirring often. Keep hot. Serve with any meat or seafood fondue.

## ❖ LEMON-TERIYAKI SAUCE ❖

*½ cup (120 ml) soy sauce*

*½ tsp ground ginger*

*¼ cup (60 ml) sugar*

*2 Tbsp lemon juice*

Combine all ingredients and bring to a boil, stirring until the sugar is dissolved. This may be served hot or cold.

## ❖ MILD CURRY SAUCE ❖

Makes about 1 cup (240 ml)

*½ medium onion, chopped*

*1 small clove garlic, minced*

*1 inch (2.5 cm) piece of ginger root, slivered*

*1 Tbsp butter*

*½ Tbsp curry powder*

*½ tsp brown sugar*

*1½ Tbsp flour*

*¼ tsp salt*

*1 cup (240 ml) chicken stock*

Sauté onion, garlic, and ginger in the butter for about 10 minutes, or until the onion is slightly browned. Stir in curry powder and sugar; continue stirring for 1 minute. Stir in flour and salt. Add chicken stock and cook gradually, stirring until the sauce is thickened. Cook over LOW heat for 10 minutes, stirring frequently. Strain. Serve hot or cold.

## ❖ MUSTARD AND SOUR CREAM ❖

Makes ½ pint (250 ml)

*1 cup (½ pint or 250 ml) sour cream*

*3 Tbsp prepared mustard*

*2 Tbsp minced scallions*

*⅛ tsp salt*

*coarsely ground black pepper*

Combine the sour cream, prepared mustard, minced scallions, salt, and pepper.

## ❖ PEPPERY TOMATO SAUCE ❖

Makes about 1½ cups (360 ml)

*14-fl-oz (420-ml) can tomato sauce*

*1 carrot, pared and grated*

*1 Tbsp butter*

*1½ tsp vinegar*

*1½ tsp sugar*

*1 tsp Worcestershire sauce*

*¼ tsp Tabasco*

Combine all ingredients; simmer 5 minutes, stirring often. Keep hot. Serve with any meat or seafood fondue.

## ❖ PINK HORSERADISH SAUCE ❖

Makes 2 cups (480 ml)

*14-fl-oz (420-ml) can tomato sauce*
*1 cup (240 ml) sour cream*
*1 Tbsp prepared horseradish*
*salt and pepper, to taste*

Fold tomato sauce slowly into the sour cream. Add horseradish and add seasonings to taste.

This makes a tangy sauce for beef fondue. Serve it chilled or warm it in a chafing dish, but be careful not to allow the mixture to boil.

## ❖ PROVENÇAL ROUILLE ❖

Makes about 3 Tbsp

*large red pepper, seeded and diced*
*½ tsp dried red chili flakes*
*2 Tbsp olive oil*
*2 cloves garlic*

Simmer all ingredients 10 to 15 minutes until the pepper and garlic are tender. Place in a blender and blend until smooth at about the consistency of soft butter.

## ❖ SAUCE AURORE ❖

Makes about ½ cup (120 ml)

*1 Tbsp ketchup* OR *chili sauce*
*½ cup (120 ml) mayonnaise*
*dash Worcestershire sauce*
*freshly ground pepper to taste*
*1 Tbsp cognac, more if desired*

Blend all ingredients gently in a bowl.

## ❖ SAUCE DIABLE ❖

Makes about 1 cup (240 ml)

*3 cloves garlic, finely chopped*
*1 medium onion, finely chopped*
*¼ cup (60 ml) corn oil*
*1 tsp cornstarch*
*¼ pickle, chopped*
*2 Tbsp white vinegar*
*½ cup (120 ml) ketchup*
*¼ cup (60 ml) Worcestershire sauce*
*½ tsp salt*
*1 tsp dry mustard*
*Tabasco sauce*

Sauté garlic and onion in the oil until soft, but not brown. Add cornstarch and cook 1 minute, stirring constantly. Add chopped pickle, vinegar, ketchup, and Worcestershire sauce. Bring to a boil, then add the remaining ingredients.

# ❖ SAUCE ORIENTALE ❖

Makes about 1½ cups (360 ml)

*8-fl-oz (240-ml) can tomato sauce with mushrooms*
*¼ cup (60 ml) soy sauce*
*¼ cup (60 ml) orange marmalade*
*2 Tbsp lemon juice*
*¼ tsp ground ginger*
*⅛ tsp garlic powder*

Combine the tomato sauce, soy sauce, orange marmalade, lemon juice, ginger, and garlic powder. Simmer 5 minutes. Keep hot.

Serve with seafood or any meat or ham fondue.

# ❖ SAUCE TARTARE DE LUXE ❖

Makes about 1 cup (240 ml)

*2 Tbsp chopped fresh chives*

*2 Tbsp finely chopped fresh parsley*

*1 Tbsp finely chopped fresh tarragon* OR *½ Tbsp dried tarragon*

*1 Tbsp finely chopped capers*

*1 Tbsp finely chopped onion*

*1 Tbsp finely minced sour pickle*

*¼ cup (60 ml) mayonnaise*

*1 clove garlic, finely minced*

*salt and freshly ground pepper*

*lemon juice (optional)*

Combine all ingredients in a bowl and mix well.

# ❖ SESAME SEED SAUCE ❖

Makes ½ cup (120 ml)

*2 Tbsp white sesame seeds*

*⅓ cup (80 ml) soy sauce, divided*

*2 Tbsp finely chopped green onion*

*1 Tbsp cider vinegar*

*2 tsp finely chopped ginger root*

*1 tsp water*

Brown the sesame seeds over MEDIUM heat in a dry heavy skillet for about 5 minutes—or until they begin to pop. Remove from heat and while still hot, crush them with a mortar and pestle, or grind at HIGH speed in a food processor or blender, adding a few drops of soy sauce.

Add the remaining soy sauce and the green onion, cider vinegar, ginger root, and water. Blend until smooth.

# ❖ SHANGHAI SWEET AND SOUR SAUCE ❖

Makes about 1½ cup (360 ml)

*½ cup (120 ml) orange juice*

*½ cup (120 ml) cider vinegar*

*½ cup (120 ml) sugar*

*2 Tbsp tomato paste*

*½ tsp sesame oil*

*3 drops Tabasco sauce*

*1 Tbsp cornstarch*

*2 Tbsp water*

Combine all ingredients—except the cornstarch and water—in a small saucepan and bring to a boil. Dissolve the cornstarch in the water; stir into the boiling sauce and continue cooking for 1 or 2 minutes.

### NOTES

If a thicker sauce is desired, add a little more cornstarch.

While this is a fairly ubiquitous sauce with chicken, fish, ham, and pork fondues, it should NOT be used with beef dishes.

# ❖ SIMPLE HOLLANDAISE SAUCE ❖

Makes ⅔ to ¾ cup (160–180 ml)

*4 oz (110 g) butter*

*2 egg yolks*

*1 Tbsp lemon juice*

*1 Tbsp water*

*¼ tsp salt*

Melt the butter but do not allow to brown. Remove from heat. Place the remaining ingredients in a blender and beat at low speed until somewhat thickened. With blender in motion, slowly add melted butter (clear liquid only, not white particles) by pouring through the hole in the cover until the mixture is thick and creamy.

### NOTE

If a thicker sauce is desired, use a third egg yolk.

# ❖ SOY-WASABI SAUCE ❖

Makes about ⅓ cup (80 ml)

*2 oz (60 ml) soy sauce*

*2 Tbsp wasabi*

Mix the soy sauce with the wasabi (Japanese horseradish). Serve at room temperature.

## ❖ SPICY HAWAIIAN SAUCE ❖

Makes about 2 cups (480 ml)

*14-fl-oz (420-ml) can crushed pineapple, undrained*
*6-fl-oz (180-ml) can tomato sauce*
*2 Tbsp vinegar*
*1 Tbsp soy sauce*
*1 tsp prepared mustard*
*⅛ tsp onion salt*

Combine the crushed pineapple, tomato sauce, vinegar, soy sauce, prepared mustard, and salt. Simmer for 15 to 20 minutes, stirring occasionally. Keep hot.

Serve with ham, chicken, seafood, pork, or lamb fondue.

## ❖ SPICY RED APPLE SAUCE ❖

Makes about 3 cups (720 ml)

*8½-oz (255-ml) can apple sauce*
*14-fl-oz (420-ml) can tomato sauce*
*¼ cup (60 ml) dark brown sugar, firmly packed*
*1 Tbsp butter*
*½ tsp allspice*
*¼ tsp ground cloves*
*⅛ tsp Tabasco sauce*

Combine the apple sauce, tomato sauce, brown sugar, butter, allspice,
cloves, and Tabasco sauce. Simmer, stirring frequently. Keep hot. Serve
with pork or ham fondue.

# ❖ SWEET AND SOUR SAUCE ❖

Makes about 2 cups (480 ml)

*¾ cup (180 ml) finely chopped onion*
*¼ cup (60 ml) finely chopped green pepper*
*2 Tbsp vegetable oil*
*1 Tbsp cornstarch*
*½ cup (120 ml) water*
*8-fl-oz (240-ml) can tomato sauce*
*2 Tbsp orange marmalade*
*2 Tbsp vinegar*
*½ tsp powdered ginger*

Cook the onion and green pepper in oil over MEDIUM heat until tender. Blend cornstarch with water and add along with the tomato sauce, orange marmalade, vinegar, and powdered ginger. Simmer 5 to 10 minutes. Keep hot. Serve with pork, ham, lamb, or chicken fondue.

# ❖ TARTAR-RELISH SAUCE ❖

Makes about 1 cup (240 ml)

*9-oz (270 ml) jar tartar sauce*
*4 tsp drained sweet relish*
*1 Tbsp mayonnaise*
*1 Tbsp capers*

Combine the tartar sauce, sweet relish, mayonnaise, and capers in a bowl and mix well.

## ❖ TERIYAKI SAUCE ❖

*½ cup (120 ml) soy sauce*

*1 clove garlic, minced*

*1 Tbsp brown sugar*

*1 tsp fresh ginger, grated*

*¼ cup (60 ml) sake\**

Combine the soy sauce, garlic, brown sugar, ginger, and sake.

*Although it isn't Japanese, dry sherry can be used in place of the sake. This sauce is delicious with any fish or meat fondue.

## ❖ TOMATO PAPRIKA SAUCE ❖

Makes about 1 cup (240 ml)

*3 Tbsp butter*

*3 Tbsp finely chopped onion*

*¼ cup (60 ml) flour*

*1 Tbsp paprika*

*3 medium tomatoes, coarsely chopped*

*salt and freshly ground pepper*

*2 Tbsp sour cream*

Melt 2 Tbsp of the butter in a saucepan and add onion. Sauté until the onion is wilted. Stir in flour and paprika. Stir in tomatoes; add salt and pepper to taste. Simmer for 15 minutes, stirring frequently. Put the sauce through the finest strainer possible, or use a food mill. Stir in the sour cream. Swirl in the remaining butter. Serve hot.

# ❖ WESTERN SAUCE ❖

Makes about 1½ cups (360 ml)

*1 cup (240 ml) Rancho sauce*
*½ cup (120 ml) ketchup*
*salt and pepper*
*Tabasco sauce*

Combine the Rancho sauce, ketchup, salt, pepper, and Tabasco sauce in a bowl.

## OTHER SAUCES AND RELISHES

Other appropriate sauces and relishes come in bottles, jars, and cans, or can be easily prepared from piquant foods.

Chop anchovies, gherkins, mushrooms, olives, or radishes and finely chop Spanish onions or scallions. Mustard can be hot, mild, sweet, or honey. Use freshly grated horseradish. Here are some possibilities.

Anchovies

Chutney

Cumberland Sauce

Gherkins

Horseradish

Horseradish Cream

Horseradish Sauce

Mayonnaise

Mushroom Ketchup

Mustard (hot, mild, or sweet)

Mustard Sauce

Olives

Onion Relish

Peanuts

Piccalilli

Pickled Mushrooms

Pickle Relish

Radishes

Scallions

Spanish Onion

Tartar Sauce

Tomato Ketchup

Tomato Mayonnaise

Vinaigrette

Worcestershire Sauce

# The Other Side of the Dish

The potato holds court.

*The cheese fondue is a meal in itself. However, many a cook feels as though something is missing if this cheese delight is the sole item on the menu.*

*The Swiss themselves tend to serve a minor meat course before or after the fondue—Bindenfleisch (smoke- or air-dried raw beef, thinly sliced and dressed with oil and vinegar) before the fondue or a little smoked ham, or perhaps sausage, after the fondue.*

*On this side of the Atlantic, conscious of the delights of a crisp salad, many cooks will offer their favorite cold vegetable mixture, usually without a pungent or heavy dressing but with just a little salt, or salt and vinegar, or simply lemon juice alone (which tends to enhance the taste of raw vegetables in contrast to the cheese flavors).*

*In addition to the vast variety of sauces used with meat fondues, a number of side dishes can be added to the table. Cranberries, for instance, make an excellent side dish, as do mixed pickles.*

*Any cooked vegetable is good with a meat fondue, and saffron or Spanish rice is especially tasty.*

*While you wait for your meal to cook, a salad to nibble is a good idea. This can consist of any variety of cold vegetables, including cherry tomatoes, chilled cauliflower florets, sweet red pepper, or any other vegetables that*

will not conflict with the sauces you have prepared for meat dipping.

On the German-speaking side of Switzerland, the potato holds court, and rösti in some of its variations is often an accompanying dish for a meat fondue. Many supermarkets carry a prepared rösti in a 15-oz (425-ml) can that may be worth considering if you're in too much of a hurry to prepare potatoes. We've included a few rösti varieties.

# ❖ KARTOFFELRÖSTI ❖

Makes 4 to 6 servings

*2 lb (0.9 kg) potatoes*
*4 Tbsp butter*
*¾ tsp salt*
*2 Tbsp hot water*

Boil potatoes in their skins, cool and peel. Shred the potatoes, or cut into julienne strips. Melt the butter in a large skillet; gradually add potatoes and salt. Cook over LOW heat, turning frequently, until the potatoes are soft and yellow.

Press the potatoes with a broad spatula into a flat cake. Sprinkle with hot water; cover and cook over LOW heat (for about 15 to 20 minutes), or until the potatoes are crusty and golden on the bottom. Shake the pan frequently to prevent scorching. If necessary, add a little more butter to prevent sticking.

Turn into a hot serving dish crusty side up; serve immediately.

# ❖ BAUERNRÖSTI ❖

Makes 4 servings

*6 potatoes*

*½ cup (120 ml) vegetable oil*

*½ tsp salt*

*pepper*

*1 small onion, finely chopped*

Boil potatoes in their skins, cool and peel; cut into julienne strips. Heat oil in a heavy skillet. Add potatoes, salt, pepper (to taste), and onion. Sauté until potatoes are golden brown.

## ❖ BERNESE RÖSTI ❖

Makes 4 to 6 servings

*2 lb (0.9 kg) potatoes*
*¼ cup (60 ml) lard*
*¾ tsp salt*
*3 slices bacon, diced*
*1 small onion, minced*
*2 Tbsp hot water*

Boil potatoes in their skins, cool and peel; cut into julienne strips. Melt lard in a heavy skillet; add potatoes and salt slowly. Cook over LOW heat, turning frequently, until potatoes are soft and yellow.

Cook bacon and onion until onion is soft. Make sure neither becomes brown.

Add bacon and onion mixture to potatoes. Press mixture with a broad spatula into a flat cake and sprinkle with hot water. Cook over LOW heat for about 15 to 20 minutes, or until potatoes are crusty and golden on the bottom. Shake skillet to prevent scorching. Turn into a hot serving dish crusty side up; serve immediately.

# ❖ CHEESE RÖSTI ❖

Makes 4 to 6 servings

*2 lb (1 kg) potatoes*
*4 Tbsp butter*
*¾ tsp salt*
*½ cup (120 ml) Swiss OR Gruyère cheese, diced*
*2 Tbsp hot water*

Boil potatoes in their skins, cool, peel, and shred. Melt butter in a heavy skillet. Add potatoes gradually, along with salt and cheese. Cook over LOW heat, turning frequently, until potatoes are soft.

Press into a flat cake with a broad spatula and sprinkle with hot water. Cover and cook over LOW heat for about 15 to 20 minutes, or until the potatoes are crusty and golden brown on the bottom. Shake the pan frequently to prevent scorching.

Turn into a hot serving dish crusty side up; serve immediately.

# Topping the Meal

Desserts aren't only for kids.

$S$*election of a dessert after a fondue should be made with care.
In Switzerland, a cheese fondue is often followed simply by a tangy fresh apple. Other cold fruit, whole or cut up in a fruit salad arrangement, makes a pleasant end to the fondue meal.*

*But if you want something different after a fondue meal—either cheese or meat—you will find a number of unusual dessert recipes in this section to test your ingenuity as a cook.*

*Before looking at post-fondue desserts, however, there are nine fondue recipes based on chocolate. Any of the nine might serve as a dessert for a nonfondue meal. They can also be served as a mid-afternoon or late-evening fondue snack, if a fondue on the sweet side is preferred to one on the tangy side.*

# ❖ FONDUE CHOCOLAT ❖

Makes 4 to 6 servings

*10 oz (280 g) chocolate*
*½ cup (120 ml) light cream*
*2 Tbsp kirsch, cognac,* OR *Cointreau*
*dunkables*

Break chocolate into pieces about 1 inch (2.5 cm) square. Combine chocolate, cream, and kirsch in a fondue pot. Place over LOW heat and stir until chocolate is melted and mixture is smooth. Keep fondue pot over LOW heat.

# ❖ FONDUE CHOCOLAT AU JUS ❖

Makes 4 to 6 servings

*14-oz (400-g) bar Toblerone chocolate (bittersweet, milk,* OR *white)*
*½ cup (120 ml) whipping cream*
*3 Tbsp fruit juice concentrate, liqueur,* OR *fruit brandy*

Separate chocolate bar into triangles; place in top of double boiler with cream. Heat over hot water, stirring constantly, until chocolate is melted and thoroughly mixed with the cream. Add juice concentrate 1 Tbsp at a time, stirring after each addition. Pour into fondue pot over LOW heat.

# ❖ FONDUE CHOCOLAT À L'ORANGE ❖

Makes 4 to 6 servings

*6 oz (170 g) bittersweet* OR *semisweet chocolate*
*¾ cup (180 ml) half-and-half cream (10%)*
*¼ cup (60 ml) Grand Marnier*
*1 tsp finely grated orange rind*

Follow directions for the Fondue Chocolat (page 138).

# ❖ NONALCOHOLIC CHOCOLATE ❖

Omit the liqueur, but add a vanilla bean to the pot. Make sure the bean stays there—do not let anyone lick it! Otherwise, follow directions for Fondue Chocolat (page 138).

# ❖ IRISH "HABIT" ❖

Dilute 1 tsp of instant coffee in 2 Tbsp of Irish whiskey to replace any other liqueur. Follow directions for Fondue Chocolat (page 138)

## ❖ CHRISTMAS GREETINGS ❖

Prepare the basic Fondue Chocolat (page 138) without any alcohol.

Dunkables should be dried fruits which should be soaked ahead of time to soften them: prunes and sultanas (dried, seedless white grapes) in rum; apricots in kirsch; and figs in cognac.

To add to the festive flavors, ice some chestnuts and add them to the dunkables.

## ❖ KWIK 'N' EASY ❖

Makes 6 servings

*1 package chocolate pudding and pie-filling mix*

*2¼ cups (540 ml) milk*

*2 Tbsp orange liqueur*

Combine the packaged chocolate pudding mix and milk in a fondue pot. Stir until smooth.

Add the orange liqueur, stirring constantly over LOW heat until the mixture thickens and comes to a boil. Boil for 2 minutes, then place over LOW heat.

## ❖ FONDUE CHOCOLAT-NOISETTE ❖

Makes 4 to 6 servings

*½ cup (120 ml) whole hazelnuts*

*8 oz (225 g) bittersweet chocolate*

*½ cup (120 ml) table cream*

*2 oz (60 ml) brandy* OR *hazelnut liqueur*

Toast the hazelnuts in a 350°F (175°C) oven for 10 to 20 minutes, turning frequently. Rub the skins off the nuts while they are still warm, then chop the nuts coarsely. Melt the chocolate in a fondue pot and add the cream, liqueur, and nuts.

## ❖ MOCHA FONDUE ❖

Makes 6 to 8 servings

*8 oz (225 g) semisweet chocolate*

*½ cup (120 ml) hot espresso* OR *strong coffee\**

*3 Tbsp granulated sugar*

*2 Tbsp butter*

*½ tsp vanilla*

Chop the chocolate coarsely. Stir the coffee with the sugar in a fondue pot over LOW heat until the sugar dissolves. Add chocolate and butter, stirring frequently until mixture is smooth. Add vanilla.

*For extra zing, put 2 Tbsp of brandy, rum, or Irish cream liqueur into the measuring cup and then add the coffee to measure ½ cup (120 ml).

## ❖ CINNAMON FONDUE ❖

Makes 4 to 6 servings

*10 oz (280 g) milk chocolate*
*½ cup (120 ml) light* OR *heavy cream*
*¼ tsp cinnamon*
*¼ tsp ground cloves*

Break the chocolate into pieces about 1 inch (2.5 cm) square. Combine with other ingredients in a fondue pot. Place over LOW heat and stir until the chocolate is melted and the mixture is smooth. Keep the fondue pot over LOW heat.

## ❖ COFFEE-CHOCK FONDUE ❖

Makes 4 to 6 servings

*10 oz (310 ml) milk chocolate*
*½ cup (120 ml) heavy cream*
*1 Tbsp instant coffee*

Break the chocolate into pieces about 1-inch (2.5-cm) square. Combine with the heavy cream and instant coffee in a fondue pot. Place over LOW heat and stir until chocolate is melted and mixture is smooth. Keep the fondue pot over LOW heat.

## ❖ COCOA FONDUE ❖

Makes 4 servings

*6 Tbsp unsalted butter*

*1 cup (240 ml) sugar*

*⅔ cup (160 ml) cocoa*

*½ cup (120 ml) evaporated milk*

*1 tsp vanilla*

Melt butter in a saucepan over LOW heat. Sift together the sugar and cocoa; stir into the butter. Stir in the evaporated milk gradually. Cook over LOW heat, stirring constantly, until the sugar is dissolved and the sauce is hot. Add the vanilla; transfer to a fondue pot for serving.

## ❖ FONDUE À L'ANGE ❖

Makes 4 servings

*4 cups (1 quart or 1 L) fresh strawberries*

*4 to 6 slices sponge cake*

*⅔ cup (160 ml) heavy cream*

*1 cup (240 ml) miniature marshmallows*

*2 Tbsp powdered sugar*

Wash and hull strawberries. Cut the cake into pieces about 1 inch (2.5 cm) square. Combine the remaining ingredients in a fondue pot. Stir until well blended and marshmallows are melted. Use strawberries and cake, alternately, as dunkables.

## ❖ WINE CUSTARD FONDUE ❖

Makes 6 to 8 servings

*4.8-oz (135-g) package egg custard mix*

*4.8-oz (135-g) package vanilla pudding and pie filling mix*

*1½ cups (360 ml) milk*

*½ tsp grated orange rind*

*1 cup (240 ml) dry white wine*

Combine the packaged mixes in a saucepan. Stir in the milk and orange rind. Cook over MEDIUM heat, stirring constantly, until the mixture thickens and comes to a boil. Boil for 1½ minutes. Reduce heat to LOW and stir in wine; transfer the mixture to a fondue pot for serving.

## ❖ BUTTERSCOTCH FONDUE ❖

Makes 2 or 3 servings

*½ cup (120 ml) dark brown sugar, well packed*

*1 Tbsp flour*

*salt*

*1 cup (240 ml) milk*

*2 Tbsp butter*

*1 tsp vanilla*

Combine sugar, flour, and a pinch of salt. Whisk in milk, gradually, until the mixture is smooth. Place on HIGH heat until the mixture comes to a boil and thickens, whisking two or three times during cooking. Stir in the butter until melted; add vanilla.

# ❖ PINEAPPLE CREAM ❖

Makes 4 to 6 servings

*19-fl-oz (570-ml) can pineapple chunks, chilled*
  *and drained*

*mint leaves*

*1½ cups (360 ml) sour cream*

*1½ cups (360 ml) light brown sugar*

In a large serving bowl, place crushed ice up to about the halfway point. Place pineapple chunks on top of the ice and garnish with mint leaves. Put sour cream and sugar in serving bowls. With fondue forks (or wooden picks) have guests pick up a pineapple chunk from the large bowl, dip the fruit in sour cream, and then in brown sugar.

## FRUIT CREAM VARIATIONS

Use mandarin or clementine orange sections in place of the pineapple.

# ❖ TAFFY APPLE MINIATURES ❖

Makes 4 to 6 servings

*8-fl-oz (240-ml) jar butterscotch sundae sauce*
*apples*
*chopped walnuts, pecans, toasted almonds*

Heat the butterscotch sauce over LOW heat in a fondue pot. Core the apples, cut them into quarters, and then in half crosswise. Dip chunks of apples into the sauce and then into a small bowl of chopped nuts.

# ❖ CHOCOLATE-CHIP ORANGES ❖

Makes 4 servings

*4 navel oranges*
*2 cups (1 pint or 500 ml) chocolate-chip ice cream, semi-frozen*

Slice the top off each orange and scoop out the fruit. Discard the white pith, membrane and excess juice. Dice orange segments and measure 1 cup (240 ml) of the diced orange.

Mix the diced orange with ice cream. Fill the orange shells and replace the top slices. Set in freezer for at least 1 hour.

# ❖ CERISES D'ALSACE ❖

Makes 4 servings

*14-fl-oz (420-ml) can black OR Bing cherries*

*¼ cup (60 ml) kirsch OR brandy*

*1 tsp lemon juice*

*sugar*

*1 Tbsp cornstarch*

*vanilla ice cream*

Drain the cherries, reserving the juice. Pit the cherries. Pour the juice into a saucepan. Pour kirsch or brandy over cherries in a mixing bowl and allow to stand until ready to use.

Set aside 2 Tbsp of cherry juice; cook the remaining juice until it is reduced by about half. Add lemon juice. Add sugar to taste. Blend cornstarch with 2 Tbsp cherry juice that has been reserved; stir into simmering sauce. Add cherries and heat thoroughly.

Serve immediately over individual portions of vanilla ice cream.

# ❖ FRAISES FLAMBÉES ❖

Makes 4 servings

*2 cups (480 ml) fresh strawberries*

*3 Tbsp kirsch*

*2 tsp butter*

*2 tsp sugar*

*juice of 1 orange*

*peel of 1 orange, diced finely*

*peel of 1 lemon, diced finely*

*1½ Tbsp Cointreau*

*1½ Tbsp cognac*

*1½ Tbsp rum*

*vanilla ice cream*

Wash, hull, and quarter the strawberries. Soak them in kirsch overnight.

Melt the butter in a chafing dish. Add sugar and cook until lightly brown. Add juice of orange and peel of orange and lemon.

Add the strawberry and kirsch mixture. Add Cointreau, cognac, and rum. Heat thoroughly.

Flame and serve over vanilla ice cream as the flame dies down.

## ❖ ORANGES D'ARABIE ❖

Makes 4 to 6 servings

*6 large oranges*
*½ cup (120 ml) shredded almonds*
*¾ cup (180 ml) shredded dates*
*⅔ cup (160 ml) orange juice*
*⅓ cup (80 ml) brandy*

Peel and slice oranges thinly. Combine with almonds and dates. Combine juice and brandy and pour over the fruit; chill thoroughly.

## ❖ FRUIT GARNISH À LA SUISSE ❖

*fruit (bananas, pineapples, peaches, pears)*
*ketchup*
*chopped almonds*

Cube or dice the fruit and combine. Season for both color and taste with ketchup. Garnish with almonds. Chill and serve.

## *Dessert Dunkables*

You can try many dunkables for dessert fondues. You might want to present your guests with a buffet table selection and let them choose their own to appeal to their palates. These dunkables are speared as you would spear bread squares for a cheese fondue, dipped into the mixture and then eaten directly from the fondue fork rather than transferred to a plate and eaten with a dessert fork, lest the hot chocolate or other mixture cling to the plate.

Of course, bread squares (particularly raisin bread and other sweet loaves) can be used for dessert dunkables. Make slices, chunks, or squares about 1 inch (2.5 cm) long or cut into 1-inch (2.5-cm) squares. Or choose small or bite-size pastries, cookies, doughnuts, or puffs. Slice cake, ladyfingers, breads, doughnuts, muffins, or Scottish oatcakes into squares or chunks. If your guests are teenagers or younger, or are dessert buffs, make up your own selection. Here are some ideas.

You could follow by dipping the dunkable into little bowls of crushed nuts or coconut.

## PASTRIES

Angel Food, Sponge, or Pound Cake

Beignets

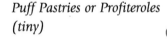

Doughnuts

Ladyfingers

Marshmallows

Muffins

Oatcakes

Pretzels

Puff Pastries or Profiteroles *(tiny)*

Shortbread or Gingerbread Cookies (small)

Sweet Breads—date bread, raisin bread, banana bread, pumpkin bread, zucchini bread

Waffles

# FRESH FRUIT

Fresh fruit is best if it has been left in the refrigerator for a day before preparing and serving. Chunks, slices, or squares about 1 inch (2.5 cm) long of various fruits work well.

Dip apple and banana slices immediately into lemon juice to prevent browning. Peel and slice kiwis; pit cherries, apricots, peaches, and pears. Core apples; peel if you wish.

Use sections of oranges, grapefruit, tangerines, or clementines; use seedless varieties or remove seeds. Choose large seedless grapes. Hull strawberries. Frozen grapes or strawberries also make good dunkables.

Use chunks of pineapple and mango and chunks or balls of melon.

*Apples (sliced thin, halved or cut into eighths)*

*Apricots (quartered)*

*Bananas (cut lengthwise then into 1-inch slices)*

*Cherries (pitted)*

*Clementines (sections)*

*Grapefruit (sections)*

*Grapes (large, seedless)*

*Kiwis (peeled and sliced)*

*Mangoes (square chunks)*

*Melons (balls or chunks)*

*Oranges (seedless, halved sections)*

*Peaches (quartered then cut into halves)*

*Pears (quartered then cut into thirds)*

*Pineapple (square chunks)*

*Raspberries*

*Strawberries*

*Tangerines (sections)*

## CANNED FRUIT

Use fruit sections or chunks well-drained. Prepare in quarters, chunks, or slices. Pit plums and other fruit as necessary.

Apricots (cut into quarters)

Cherries (sour, sweet, Bing, white, or maraschino)

Crab Apples (slices)

Grapefruit (sections cut into halves)

Kumquats

Mandarin Oranges (slices)

Peaches (slices)

Pears (cut into quarters)

Pineapple (chunks)

Plums (pitted and quartered)

## DRIED FRUIT

Choose from the many possible combinations you can imagine.

Apples

Apricots

Banana Chips

Cherries

Dates

Figs

Peaches (cut into halves)

Pears (cut into halves)

Pineapple

Plums

Prunes

Sultanas

# Prost!

## What do you drink after a fondue?

*Just as there is controversy about fondues, so there is often heated discussion as to what should or should not be drunk with them.*

*Basically, the Swiss say, cold drinks do not harmonize with hot or warm cheese fondues. They serve kirsch at room temperature (about 68°F or 20°C) along with, or after, a fondue. Elsewhere a dry white wine (perhaps the wine used to make the fondue), or even a dry rosé, has become acceptable as a cheese fondue accompaniment. So experiment for yourself; drink to your own taste.*

*With a meat fondue, Burgundy is the drink—though here again you may serve a beverage of your own choice. If you are a white wine aficionado, make sure it's a dry wine. With a rabbit type of dish, cold beer is the best drink—some say—but dry white wine is not out of place.*

*The end of the meal in Switzerland is usually a hot drink—coffee or tea. True fondue enthusiasts prefer tea.*

*An interesting group of hot after-meal drinks exists. We provide a small selection of recipes, any of which would do well as a post-fondue libation. Some might even accompany that delectable dish.*

# ❖ GLÖGG ❖

Makes 4 to 6 servings

4 cardamom seeds
½ cup (120 ml) raisins
3 whole cloves
2 cinnamon sticks OR ¼ tsp powdered cinnamon
1-L bottle dry red wine
¼ cup (60 ml) sugar
2 cups (480 ml) brandy OR bourbon

Remove cardamom seeds from pods, discarding the pods, and crush the seeds. Add crushed cardamom seeds, raisins, cloves, and cinnamon to the wine in a large saucepan and allow it to stand for 24 hours. Heat until the mixture steams, shortly before serving—but DO NOT BOIL. Then add sugar (to taste) and liquor. Serve hot in heavy heat-proof glasses or mugs.

## GLÖGG VARIATIONS

# CHERRY GLÖGG

Follow the directions for Glögg, but use Cherry Kijafa instead of wine and only 2 Tbsp sugar.

# ❖ HOT ORANGE WINE ❖

Makes 4 to 6 servings

*large orange*
*1½ cups (360 ml) water*
*½ lb (225 g) sugar*
*1-L bottle red wine*
*1 thin slice of orange per drink*

Juice the orange; set aside half of the juice.

Heat the other half of the juice and the water in a large saucepan. Dissolve the sugar in the remaining juice, using a second pan. Add the warmed juice and water mixture to the sugared juice and boil for 10 minutes.

Heat the wine until it bubbles. Add the wine to the juice mixture.

Serve in heavy heat-proof glasses or mugs that have been warmed. Float a thin slice of orange atop each glass or mug.

## ❖ TODDY TEMPEST ❖

Makes 4 servings

*2 cups (480 ml) orange juice*

*1 cup (240 ml) cranberry juice cocktail*

*¼ cup (60 ml) sugar*

*1 tsp whole cloves*

*3-inch (7.5-cm) piece cinnamon stick*

*1 tsp grated orange rind*

*4 slices of orange*

*4 whole cloves as decoration*

Combine all ingredients, except the sliced orange, in a saucepan. Place over LOW heat and bring to the boiling point. Reduce heat and simmer for 5 minutes; strain. Pour into a heated bowl or pitcher. Stick additional cloves into orange slices and float atop the toddy. Serve hot in heavy heat-proof glasses or mugs.

## ❖ IRISH COFFEE ❖

*hot coffee*

*1 fl oz. (30 ml) Irish whiskey per person*

*1 tsp Kahlua per person*

*whipped cream*

Pour the coffee, whiskey, and Kahlua into an Irish coffee glass or mug. Stir; then float whipped cream on top.

# ❖ MULLED WINE ❖

Makes 4 to 6 servings

*1-L bottle dry red wine*

*cinnamon*

*cloves*

*nutmeg*

*sugar*

Add dry ingredients, to taste, to the wine and heat in a large saucepan. Serve hot in heavy heat-proof glasses or mugs.

# METRIC EQUIVALENTS

## Liquid or Capacity Measures

1 gallon = 4 quarts = 128 fl oz

2 quarts = ½ gallon = 1.8 L = 64 fl oz

4 cups = 1 quart = 960 ml = 32 fl oz

2 cups = 480 ml = 1 pint = 16 fl oz

1¾ cups = 420 ml = 14 fl oz

1½ cups = 360 ml = 12 fl oz

1¼ cups = 300 ml = 10 fl oz

1 cup = 240 ml = ½ pint = 8 fl oz

¾ cup = 180 ml = 6 fl oz

⅔ cup = 160 ml = 5.3 fl oz

½ cup = 120 ml = 4 fl oz

⅓ cup = 80 ml = 2.6 fl oz

¼ cup = 60 ml = 2 fl oz

⅛ cup = 30 ml = 1 fl oz

## Tablespoons and Teaspoons

2 Tbsp = ⅛ cup = 30 ml = 1 fl oz

1 Tbsp = 3 tsp = 15 ml

1 tsp = 5 ml

¾ tsp = 4 ml (3.75 ml)

½ tsp = 2.5 ml

¼ tsp = 1 ml (1.25 ml)

⅛ tsp = 0.5 ml = pinch

dash = less than a pinch or ¹⁄₁₆ tsp

## Weight

2.2 lb = 1 kg

2 lb = 900 g or 0.9 kg (908 g)

1½ lb = 675 g (681 g)

1 lb = 16 oz = 450 g (454 g)

15 oz = 420 g

14 oz = 400 g (392 g)

13 oz = 365 g (364 g)

12 oz = ¾ lb = 335 g (336 g)

11 oz = 305 g (308 g)

10 oz = 280 g

9 oz = 250 g (252 g)

8 oz = ½ lb = 225 g (227 g)

7 oz = (200 g)

6 oz = 168 g (170 g)

5 oz = 140 g

4 oz = ¼ lb = 110 g (112 g)

3 oz = 85 g

2 oz = 55 g (56 g)

1 oz = 30 g (28 g)

½ ounce = 15 g (14 g)

## Length

1 inch = 2.5 cm (2 or 3 cm)

½ inch = 1.25 cm

## Abbreviations

cm = centimeter(s), fl oz = fluid ounces, g = gram(s), kg = kilogram(s), L = liter(s), lb = pound(s), ml = milliliters, oz = ounces, Tbsp = tablespoon(s), tsp = teaspoon(s)

# INDEX